Awakening in Asia

BAILEY MARKS

with Shirley Mewhinney

HERE'S LIFE PUBLISHERS, INC.

P.O. BOX 1576
SAN BERNARDINO, CA 92402

Scripture quotations, unless otherwise identified, are from the New American Standard Bible, copyright © The Lockman Foundation, 1960, 1962, 1963, 1968, 1971, 1972, 1973, and used by permission.

AWAKENING IN ASIA
by Bailey Marks
with Shirley Mewhinney

Published by Here's Life Publishers, Inc.
the publishing ministry of
Campus Crusade for Christ International
P.O. Box 1576, San Bernardino, CA 92402

Library of Congress Catalog card 81-67815
ISBN 0-86605-029-9
HLP Product No. 40-05-07

DEDICATED

TO

THE STAFF OF THE

ASIA-SOUTH PACIFIC AREA OF AFFAIRS

CAMPUS CRUSADE FOR CHRIST INTERNATIONAL

whose wholehearted commitment to God

and

faithful service in this movement

have been a constant source of personal

joy and encouragement.

They have made this book possible.

It is their story!

TABLE OF CONTENTS

FOREWORD

This book bears my name as its author; however, that is misleading. No one can claim authorship of the true stories of transformed lives and miracles that are recorded within these pages. Our prayer target was that God would use the staff of Campus Crusade for Christ to help saturate this great Asian continent with the message of His love and forgiveness during 1980. As staff members, working with other members of the body of Christ, fanned out across the various Asian countries, I believe we can safely say that an unprecendented spiritual awakening began on this continent.

I have had the great privilege of directing our ministry in Asia and the South Pacific area of affairs where these staff members have faithfully carried out their responsibilities with great dedication and perseverance. What a joy it has been to compile and record the historic things God has done through these "fireseeds" – Spirit-filled men and women who are now entering an even more exciting decade with even greater potential – the 1980's: the Decade of Destiny.

Rejoice with us for the great things God has done. Sing praises to Him and give Him the glory for the estimated 11 million people in Asia who indicated they had personally prayed to receive Christ into their hearts by faith during 1980.

Bailey Marks
Baguio, Philippines

PREFACE

In February 1981, I was privileged to meet for an entire week with Bailey Marks, director of affairs for Asia, and national directors and representatives from 43 Asian countries.

Hour after hour, day after day, individual reports of God's supernatural working in all of those countries, through the various Here's Life campaigns and strategies, thrilled my heart. They brought tears to my eyes again and again, as I lifted my heart to praise and give thanks to God for this dramatic demonstration of His supernatural harvest throughout the entire continent of Asia.

It is no exaggeration to say that never before in the history of the church – and to God be all the glory, honor and praise – has such a dramatic demonstration of the power of God resulted in such an unprecedented harvest.

You will read in *Awakening in Asia* how more than 200 million people were confronted with the claims of Christ through the Here's Life "I Found It" campaign – "I found new life in Jesus Christ" – and how, as a result, more than 11 million people have indicated their desire to receive and follow Christ. These are only the recorded decisions. It is estimated that the total could actually be double or perhaps several times that number. Only God knows. Even that which we have seen and heard personally is beyond our comprehension. We frankly bow in reverence, awe, worship and praise. This is God's doing, and it is marvelous in our eyes.

One cannot read the events reported in this book without being drawn closer to Christ and experiencing a dramatic expansion of vision and increased faith. I pray that God will speak to all who read this book in the way that He spoke to me when I heard the oral reports, and later when I reviewed the manuscript.

As you read *Awakening in Asia*, be prepared to have God speak to your heart in an unusual way. Stand ready to obey His instructions – to join these, about whom this story is told, in helping to reach the world for Christ in obedience to our Lord's command:

"I have been given all authority in heaven and earth. Therefore go and make disciples in all nations, baptizing them into the name of the Father and of the Son and of the Holy Spirit, and then teach these new disciples to obey all the commands I have given you; and be sure of this – that I am with you always, even to the end of the world" (Matthew 28:18-20, Living Bible).

Bill Bright
President and Founder
Campus Crusade for Christ
International

ACKNOWLEDGMENTS

In compiling this book, a number of people assisted me. I would like to acknowlege those listed below for whose contribution I am especially grateful.

I wish to express my deep appreciation to Shirley Mewhinney who worked hand in hand with me to produce this book.

I would also like to thank three other Campus Crusade for Christ staff members for whose help I am very thankful: Mary Daniels who provided the information for Chapter 6, and Vickie Kyte and Gail Porter for their editing of the manuscript.

INTRODUCTION

Christians today look out on the most winnable world ever to exist. There are many more winnable today than in the days of David Livingston and William Carey. The missionary prayers and labors of the last 200 years are bearing fruit. Whitened harvest fields stretch away on every side.

Yet, some Christians do not see the true situation. Standing by the well in Samaria, our Lord said to His disciples, "Do you not say, four months more and then comes harvest?" The disciples thought they were looking on fields ready for sowing. The Lord knew the fields were ready for harvest. That is the precise condition today.

Bailey Marks' *Awakening in Asia* is essential reading for Christians across America and around the world. It is a good antidote for the loss of nerve and the indifference which have swept over some denominations. The fact is that missions are hungry for the gospel. Many secularists, Marxists, Hindus, Muslims, and Buddhists want new life. They listen avidly as they hear of new life in Jesus Christ.

They not only listen, they act. To be sure, not all act. Some scoff. Some turn away. Some accept Christ and then forget Him. But some – praise God – go on to form Christ Groups, fellowships which meet regularly to read and obey the Word. Many continue in the apostolic teaching and prayers. A smaller number ask for baptism and in existing congregations or found new ones.

Campus Crusade teams presenting Christ as the way to new life, and operating in many Asian countries, have awakened unexpected response. Going to villages where the people are said to be "utterly indifferent to Christianity," they have seen dozens and in some cases, hundreds receive Christ. In Muslim populations, where "everyone knows" they will not listen to the preaching of Christ, Campus Crusade teams have had the joy of hearing leading men declare that they have received Christ. In some cases, House Fellowships of such believers have been established.

The film *Jesus,* which uses, almost exclusively, the words of St. Luke's Gospel, has been wonderfully blessed by God to the opening of people's hearts. In Bangladesh the words are taken from the Bengali version of Luke's Gospel. In Nepal the words are Nepali; in Thailand they are Thai, and in Korea, Korean. Millions have seen the film, been powerfully moved by it and have asked that it be shown again. Of these millions, many thousands have declared that they opened their hearts to Christ and now believe in Him.

Awakening in Asia is an exact title. Mr. Marks tells of an *awakening to Christ.* He shows us wheat fields which are "already white to harvest." He makes us long for more of the golden grain to be carried into the Master's Barn. Chapter 9 is titled "Awakening Leads to Church Growth." In many cases it does exactly that. Nepal is a resistant nation. It is illegal for a person to preach or share his faith in public. The law prohibits anyone changing his religion. Men are jailed for preaching baptism or being baptized. In 1978 there were, nonetheless, 8,000 Christians in that mountainous state. By the end of 1980, after the showing of the film, *Jesus,* and ardent campaigns by Campus Crusade teams, there were 15,000 Christians.

In open nations such as South Korea and the Philippines, the numbers of baptized believers have multiplied in striking fashion. Awakening does lead to church growth.

In 1981 Campus Crusade's international leaders, assembled in Baguio, north of Manila, listened to the directors from all the Asian countries in which work is carried on. As the size of the awakening became apparent, they thanked God, and then asked, "What does God want us to do *now?*" After much prayer and discussion, they agreed to set a goal of establishing *a million house fellowships* in which those who have received Christ into their hearts and have determined to accept the Bible as their rule of faith and practice meet together to learn of Christ, pray to

God, and encourage one another. This is sound missionary strategy, an excellent first step.

Christians in the West and around the world should praise God that the setting of such a goal is possible. They should pray that God will empower Campus Crusade and many other missionary organizations to achieve it. House fellowships are an intermediate step. Baptism is not administered in them, nor is bread broken. House fellowships should speedily go on to become house churches, hopefully in whatever branch of the Church Universal that is strong in that region. If there is no branch there, then like the churches in Rome, which Paul names in the 16th chapter of Romans, believers would become full Christians ahead of the arrival of the already established branches of the Church.

Bailey Marks, in his vivid descriptions, often mentions the glorious work of the missions and churches which have labored in all these lands. The ripened harvest fields are their sowings, blessed by the Holy Spirit. His book will stimulate the missionary movement in all denominations and all lands. "What you have done," Marks shouts, "is bearing wonderful fruit. Thrust in more laborers, train more harvesters. Pray more fervently. Give more sacrificially. Multiply missions and churches. This is the day which the Lord has made."

Here at the School of Missions we know from our research associates – national leaders and missionaries from scores of countries – that in many lands Christians look out on amazingly winnable populations. To be sure, some populations still reject the gospel, but these must not be allowed to obscure the millions who can today be discipled.

Today, despite resistant populations, Macedonias stretch away on every side. Today all mission organizations and churches ought to be setting goals for the "yet to believe" for whom God has made them responsible. Their goals may not be "a million house fellowships," but rather a hundred percent increase in membership, or the establishment in the next five years of 300 new congregations in a population where 70 are now seen. Goal-oriented management is essential strategy for most missionary societies.

Awakening in Asia will open closed eyes, strengthen weak knees, and infuse courage in quaking hearts. It is one of the most significant books on world evangelization to come off the press in many years.

Donald McGavran
School of World Mission
Fuller Theological Seminary
Pasadena, CA

PART I
Fireseeds

CHAPTER ONE

The Korean Explosion (Prayer)

What had begun as a late afternoon shower turned into an unseasonal downpour. Donning my raincoat, I ran from my hotel to the bus that would take me and 40 platform guests to Yoido Plaza. In spite of the huge crowd that had gathered the night before, I was apprehensive. A downpour like this might keep people away.

The movement of traffic was slow. I had plenty of time to reminisce about the past two fantastic days. I was in awe over all that God was doing. Two million people snugly packed onto a one-mile slab of concrete runway. I had never seen two million people at one time. Thousands could be distinguished as individuals, but thousands more blurred into a sea of joyful motion–bobbing, singing, praying, swaying–black hair, black eyes, broad smiling faces.

Many walked for miles to get there, and then sat for hours on the concrete. After the three- to four-hour sessions, hundreds of thousands of people walked back home again. More than a million stayed to pray all night.

The first time I saw a million people walking for miles to hear about Jesus was in Korea a few years back. And here I was again...on this bus wondering, *Will they come tonight?* It was raining and raining hard.

Long before I could see them, I could hear the strong, even cadence of a Korean evangelist leading the people in prayer. And there they were–two million of them, drenched, but with beaming faces. I could hear them singing and praising. That night the crowd had become a moving sea of brightly-colored umbrellas. Beneath each umbrella were at least three jubilant Christians.

Two million believers alternately stood and sat, praising God in spite of an absolute downpour. I had seen the Christians of Korea demonstrate their fervent commitment time and time again.

People from all walks of life came to Yoido Plaza in Seoul, Korea, to participate in this history-making occasion: the culmination of Here's Life, Korea, the '80 World Evangelization crusade (HLK-'80 WEC). At the conclusion of the four nights of evening rallies held August 12-15, 1980, we discovered that a cumulative total of 10.5 million people had gathered. Total attendance of both evening and daytime meetings conducted from August 11-16 exceeded 16.3 million.

At one of the evening meetings, 2,700,000 people formed what we believed to be the largest gathering in the history of Christianity. And, as far as my associates and I can recall from the pages of history, this may well have been the largest meeting of any kind ever held.

Plans for this mammoth Crusade began in 1977 when a group of Korean evangelists announced their intention to host the World Evangelization Crusade in August, 1980. After 18 months of preparation, that committee realized they needed assistance to turn their plans into reality. Consequently, they approached Dr. Joon Gon Kim, national director of Korea Campus Crusade for Christ (and recently-appointed director for Campus Crusade for Christ International's East Asia area of affairs), requesting that he serve as executive chairman of the Crusade. They knew him to be a man of great evangelistic vision with an unusual ability to motivate, organize and involve the thousands of Christians who would be required to implement their plans.

After explaining that he was already preparing to conduct the Here's Life, Korea campaign, Dr. Kim agreed to unite the existing for '80 WEC and his own strategy into one great evangelistic thrust. Thus, the '80 World Evangelization Crusade became the culmination of Here's Life, Korea, the nationwide evangelistic saturation plan.

Without fully realizing the vast implications and objections of such a statement, Dr. Kim freely announced that he believed God would bring two million people to the evening rallies of this four-day Crusade. Many Christians were skeptical. Korean pastors and evangelists questioned such a large figure. The leadership of Korea Campus Crusade for Christ were hesitant. Even Dr. Kim's wife said, "You shouldn't have mentioned the number 'two million'!"

After the crowds cleared from Yoido Plaza, skeptics and supporters alike admitted that God had indeed brought more than two million people for the four nights of the giant Crusade.

Dr. Kim, the man God had selected for this herculean task of vision and implementation, had been prepared in an unusual way.

By his own admission, 40 years ago Dr. Kim was a nominal Christian. Reared in a strict Confucianist home, he first heard about Jesus Christ as a third-grade student in primary school. During his teenage years, he became interested in Christianity and sought out a Christian church to attend. It was there he committed his life to Christ, and became active in the church. This interest lasted throughout his school years and early married life.

Then came the Korean War. "The starting point of my real Christian life began when I faced persecution and death under the Communist occupation," testifies Dr. Kim. He and his family took refuge on Chido Island at the southern tip of Korea. Native partisans and guerrillas began to invade and confiscate property, killing individuals and families indiscriminately. No law existed, and all means of escape from the island were cut off.

At family devotions one night, Dr. Kim's devout Christian wife prayed that the family might be prepared to meet the death which seemed inevitable. That very night, Dr. Kim and his wife and father were awakened about 2 a.m. by a pounding on their door. They were trussed up and taken to the mountains to be killed.

"Our executioners were fellow villagers who had joined the Communists," recalls Dr. Kim, "and they began with my father. Just a stone's throw away from me, my father was struck on the head several times and fell dead. Then my wife, trying to keep back her tears, said goodbye to me and said she would see me in heaven. Before my eyes, she was brutally killed."

Dr. Kim was beaten repeatedly with a club until he lost consciousness and was left for dead. More than 2,000 people were murdered that night with clubs, stones and bamboo spears, but

Dr. Kim remained alive. As soon as he was able, he rushed home for his four-year-old daughter, and together they fled into the mountains.

"I am told that I was the only survivor among those whom the Communists had marked for death," he states. (Later, additional attempts were made on his life—from the time he felt a sword blade at his throat to the day he was tied in a sack to be thrown from a cliff into the sea. Each time, God intervened.)

Dragging with exhaustion, Dr. Kim and his daughter managed to keep on the run, hiding for three weeks in mountain caves along the coast. Dr. Kim recalls, "I was almost dead physically and at times could not move to help my little girl who was dying from hunger and longing for her mother. My consciousness came and went for days at a time.

"I was also dead psychologically, because I had no hope. There seemed to be no way of escape.

"But the most serious thing was my spiritual condition. I had stopped praying or expecting God to answer, and I had no desire for eternal life. I lost sight of God, and within my soul I was complaining and trying to cut myself off from Him. I experienced the total despair and darkness of spiritual death, which was a feeling of complete separation from God. It was unbearable."

Then a strange thing happened. "Suddenly I realized that my lips had begun to move in prayer to God," relates Dr. Kim. "That prayer was begun on my lips by the Holy Spirit, and ended in my heart. At that moment I passed from death to life. As I turned to my Savior, great peace and joy sprang from my heart like a river. My hatred for the Communists vanished, and there burned in my heart a desire to please God, to glorify His name and to do His will.

"I began to pray for the Communist whom I hated most—the leader who had beaten me and killed my family. I called his name and asked for God's grace and love and for forgiveness of his sin." As Dr. Kim prayed by name for all his enemies, his strength was restored.

Experiencing a new freedom from fear, hatred and death, Dr. Kim was able to stand, take his daughter by the hand and leave the cave. He headed straight to his enemy's home. When the Communist came to the door, he was greatly startled to see a man whom he believed to be dead.

Dr. Kim gently, bravely explained that he had come in the name of Jesus to express his love for the man. Overwhelmed, the man and his wife hid Dr. Kim and his daughter in their home that night. As Dr. Kim proceeded to share with his would-be murderer about the love of God and the forgiveness of sin through Jesus Christ, the Communist leader wept in repentance for his sins and became a new man in Christ.

At great risk, he continued to feed and protect Dr. Kim for several days. In time, more than 30 of the leader's fellow Communists in that village made decisions for Christ. This man is now a faithful witness for Christ, serving as a deacon in a small Presbyterian church. "We still pray for one another every day," comments Dr. Kim.

Imagine the faith, courage and supernatural love required for Dr. Kim to go back to that village. He went to find the men who had tried to kill him – the murderers of his father and his wife. And his goal was to confront them with the love of Jesus Christ. Obviously, that session with the Lord in the cave was a turning point in Dr. Kim's life. Since then, he has been used of God in a way very few people have been used in this century.

Dr. Kim's leadership in the Here's Life, Korea-'80 World Evangelization Crusade is an example of how God continues to use this man of great faith.

Although the largest, this crusade was not the first such gathering hosted by Seoul Christians. In 1973 on its final day, the Billy Graham Evangelistic Crusade brought together more than one million people. During the massive evening rallies of Explo '74, an evangelistic crusade sponsored by Campus Crusade for Christ, one evening audience exceeded 1.5 million people. In 1977 more large meetings were conducted by Korean evangelists.

Ordinarily, finding a place to hold such gatherings would be a problem. Because of the tension between North and South Korea following the Korean War, the South Korean government built auxiliary landing strips in many parts of the country. Yoido Plaza, located on an island in the Han River on the southern edge of Seoul, is one such landing strip. It consists of 3.96 million square meters of pavement. A Korean who customarily sits on the floor in his home, can easily sit in an area of one square meter, about a square yard. So, it is possible for four million people to gather quite comfortably at one time on this plaza.

Recent history of the Korean church shows that God is doing unusual things there. This small country has been singled out to receive great spiritual blessing. A "fireseed" has been ignited resulting in a phenomenal spiritual flame among her 37 million people.

There are many forces behind every great spiritual awakening. According to Dr. J. Edwin Orr, considered by many to be the foremost authority on the history of spiritual awakening and revival, the igniting force is that of prayer. Today prayer continues to undergird the tremendous spiritual blessing and harvest being reaped so bountifully across South Korea.

In 1907 a spiritual awakening began in Korea, mainly in the north. Most feel that this awakening was in direct answer to the effectual, fervent prayers of God's people there. Since that awakening the Korean church has been known as a praying church.

Much has been written about the great growth of the Korean church. Since Explo '74 it has expanded by 33% and the rate has accelerated even more since HLK-'80 WEC. It is the common persuasion of the Korean Christians that this has happened because they have prayed faithfully.

The prayer life of a Korean Christian is radically different from that of a Christian in most any other country. For decades, churches across this nation have become prayer chapels early each morning as people fill the sanctuaries to pray for their country. Following the Korean War this emphasis intensified and has not subsided. It is beautiful to hear church bells ringing each morning. The enjoyment is multiplied when you realize that this commitment to prayer is occurring at the same time in every city and in countless villages up and down the country.

The Korean Christians, not content with only early morning prayer sessions, have added other dimensions to their national prayer life. All-night prayer meetings, held each Friday night, and mountains set aside for prayer are just two of these additional observances.

Prayer mountains have been established throughout the country. As you approach these actual mountains, owned by churches and dedicated to prayer, and begin climbing you find yourself in the company of Koreans who are carrying Bibles and plastic water containers. They are coming to claim their "prayer tunnel," where they will pray and fast for 1 to 20 days. There is a waiting list for these small, totally bare, 3′ x 3′ x 6′ concrete boxes buried horizontally in the side of the mountain. A wooden door allows the occupant total privacy with his Lord. Most people bring candles or flashlights so they can see to read their Bible or write down their prayer requests. In the winter, each person must dress to survive the extreme cold in the small cubicles which are without benefit of a heating system.

As you walk along the tree-lined paths on the mountainside, you can hear voices of people praying. Even while alone, Korean Christians pray aloud, not silently. They mean business with God when they come to the prayer mountain, and as they pray, they continually bring before Him their desire for personal holiness, national and worldwide evangelization, and reunification with North Korea. They are convinced that their hope as a nation lies in Christ.

This customary prayer emphasis took on the form of a detailed strategy in the preparation of KLK-'80 WEC. It included a 40-day national prayer and fasting campaign February 10 to March 20, 1980, and a climactic three-day prayer and fasting rally at Hanul Mountain Prayer Center February 28 through March 1. Twenty thousand Christian leaders and laymen participated. In addition, in each of the 208 rural districts across Korea, large prayer and fasting rallies were held on March 1, Korea's Independence Day. During the 10 months of preparation, the district prayer committees held a total of 13,434 prayer meetings.

A list of 87 specific HLK-'80 WEC prayer requests was developed. Eighty-seven prayer cards were then printed and assembled in sets. Every card included one prayer request in each of six categories: a specific HLK-'80 WEC prayer request, one city and county of North Korea, mainland China, one nation of the world, the one or more persons with whom the one praying would share Christ, and that the praying person's local church would double its membership as a result of the campaign.

Thousands of sets were distributed across Korea and one prayer card from a set was given to each Christian. Thus, almost every adult Christian and thousands of young people and children across Korea were given the responsibility for claiming victory for the six requests on their cards.

God is pouring out His Spirit in Korea in a wonderful way in answer to these prayers. These Christians take God seriously. They have a great vision and believe Him for the evangelization of their nation. They also plan to take their place in the evangelization of the world. Here's Life, Korea-'80 World Evangelization Crusade was a major stepping stone toward turning their vision into reality.

Here's Life, Korea followed a plan unlike most other evangelistic campaigns around the world. The entire nation held simultaneous campaigns in every city and village. Almost a million campaign workers were trained to effectively communicate their faith through Campus Crusade's mediated training units. This is an electronic package consisting of a slide projector and cassette player with more than 30 hours of audio-visual training. Within a few hours the mediated training unit can equip a layman or student to train others in how to share their faith and disciple those who become believers.

"Korea is a small country geographically and there are less than 40 million people," Dr. Kim explains. "Many times before, areas of the country have been saturated, such as at Explo '74. However, because of the use this time of mass media and nationwide training, all of Korea was saturated." He added, "The dynamics of mobilizing the entire nation at one time was warmly received by national leadership."

The simultaneous campaigns followed the standard Here's Life evangelistic format, beginning with, "I found it!" This aroused Korea's curiosity. Then the people heard about new life in Jesus Christ. Surveys indicate that 80% of them became aware that they could find that new life.

In preparation for the Here's Life, Korea media campaign, 988,600 Christians had been trained in personal evangelism and discipleship. As a result, when these trained workers went out to share Christ with those who responded to the "I Found It!" campaign, more than one million people indicated decisions for Christ.

During that crusade, 12 major seminars and 50 geographical church conferences were held for four hours each day across Seoul. An estimated 100,000 people participated in these conferences led by more than 80 Korean and foreign speakers.

The goal of having two million people attend the evangelistic rallies on Yoido Plaza was reached by encouraging one million Christians to bring one non-Christian each with them. As a result, on the first night alone, it is estimated that more than one million individuals stood up indicating they had prayed by faith to invite Christ into their lives. During the next two evenings an additional half million people responded positively to the claims of Christ, making a total of more than 1.5 million Koreans accepting Christ by faith.

Also, on the third evening, following a message on how to be filled with the Holy Spirit by faith, an estimated 1.8 million people indicated they had claimed by faith the empowering of the Holy Spirit in their lives.

A highlight for Korean Christians occurred on the final evening when a three-part challenge to become involved in missions was given. Because of the strong desire of the Korean church to become a sending nation and to help evangelize the world, Christians were asked to: (1) pray and help provide finances for missionaries, (2) dedicate their children to serve as missionaries – praying for them and encouraging them to commit their lives to His service, and (3) serve as missionaries themselves in foreign lands for at least one year.

In response to this challenge, more than one million people stood, indicating their desire and willingness to be involved in one or more of these ways. It is estimated that more than 300,000 of these made serious commitments to the Lord to serve overseas.

Since that challenge was given, the HLK-'80 WEC office has received at least ten telephone calls or letters every day requesting information as to how to prepare to go to foreign lands. Parents have opened special savings accounts for the children they dedicated. People on the streets of Seoul inquire of both staff members and volunteers how they can fulfill these commitments. The effective utilization of this vast manpower source is one of the great challenges of the next few years.

We heard thousands of stories of spiritual blessings during July and August in Korea. I am sure there are a thousand times as many stories that we did not hear. God faithfully answered the prayers of His people, and lives were changed as the following stories indicate.

A 70-year-old woman was hit by a cleaning car while she was praying in the rain during one of the all-night prayer meetings. We were filled with sorrow to hear that she died a few hours later. During her funeral, several of our staff members talked with her three daughters and sons-in-law to offer comfort. They found them rejoicing. The family explained to our staff, "Her death was by God's arrangement. She has been praying that she would die praying for the evangelization of our country. Her total assets amounted to around $70,000, including a $55,000 home and $6,000 cash. Her daughters gave all of her wealth to a struggling church in their area.

But that wasn't the end of this woman's influence. A street sweeper who witnessed the fatal accident invited Jesus Christ into his life. Although her death was tragic to him, as she died her face appeared to him divine and full of hope. "I saw God in her death," he said. And he wanted to experience the same peace and joy he had seen in her.

A student related, "I became a new person by God's grace during the Here's Life campaign. Before, I had my own way of living but I was always unsure of myself. Now I am different and so happy. I have begun to read the Bible, and I want to share the happiness and joy I found in the Lord with my friends."

Another student shared, "When I arrived home from the Here's Life rally I was very tired. But miracles had happened in my home. My brother, who was very violent and rebellious, had become a Christian through the messages he heard during the daytime conferences. His life was changed. My parents had attended the evening rallies and had also received Christ as their Savior and Lord. I praise Him because now my whole family is faithfully attending church."

A volunteer reported, "I thank the Lord for the chance to be a part of the Here's Life campaign, I was pasting Here's Life posters on the walls along the streets, and I was arrested and taken to the police station. I had unknowingly put the posters on someone's private wall. I imagined how the Apostle Paul felt when he was in prison, and I prayed for the policemen as I waited for them to release me."

"Here's Life, Korea was marvelous for me," exclaimed a young worker. "I worked where lost items were reported. One lady came to our office looking for something she couldn't find. When she found we had it, she was so grateful she gave us three thousand *won* ($5,000/U.S.). Since we could not reject her kind offer, we accepted the money and discussed how to use it.

"Soon, another young lady came to us and told us she had lost everything while she was praying. She did not even have enough money to return to her home town. When we heard her story, we recognized that we had God's provision for her. If she had three thousand *won,* she could go home. As we gave her the money which had been given to us, we could see God's particular love and plan for our lives moment by moment."

"I saw the great power of our Lord through Here's Life, Korea and the all-night prayer meetings at Yoido Plaza," related an enthusiastic participant. "God worked in a wonderful way in healing people physically. One crippled man rose up and walked. Also, I have had stomach trouble for a long time, but when I believed His power, my stomach gained complete recovery under the treatment of the 'doctor', Jesus Christ! Even though a heavy rain fell to dampen the people, none of my group caught a bad cold."

One student's response was, "The gathering of two million at Yoido Plaza did not sound realistic. I could not comprehend such a large crowd of people, so I went to see for myself. God poured out His blessings on me the first day of the week. Praying for 100,000 volunteers to become His missionaries was the request on my prayer card.

"As I prayed, I decided that first I must dedicate my life to God's service and pray with a believing heart. My prayer request became reality when countless saints stood to dedicate their lives as missionaries.

A university student reported, "In the early morning we had prayer meetings and read the training textbook, *How to Experience God's Love and Forgiveness.* Then, we started to pray and confess our sins. As we were writing down those sins, a 51-year-old man began to weep bitterly. He confessed his sins and asked the Lord to come into his life.

"We then learned he was a drunkard. He had not wanted to attend Here's Life, but because of his daughter's insistence, he did come this morning. As God's love and forgiveness became real to him after receiving Christ, he took a bottle of liquor from his suitcase and threw it away. His face reflected a special blend of joy and salvation."

The powerful public address system at the evening rallies disturbed the sleep of many people residing on Yoido Island. Because they could not sleep, they came to the rally to find out what it was about. As a result, literally hundreds of Yoido residents became Christians.

Here's Life, Korea-'80 World Evangelization Crusade is considered to be a turning point in the spiritual life of this country – a dramatic answer to the prayers of her people, a result of the zealous commitment of an army of believers. More than 90% of South Korea's 18,000 churches participated in this phenomenal event. An estimated 80,000 Christians were directly involved in the organizational structure that made it happen.

God was glorified during these unbelievable days and He poured His blessings upon this land when a total of 2.5 million people indicated they had prayed to receive Christ into their lives. The local church has already reaped tremendous benefits and will continue to do so for years to come.

Beginning as a "fireseed" of prayer many years ago, the awakening of the Korean nation has now exploded to serve as an example to Christians all across Asia and around the world. It has given them a vision and strengthened their faith to pray and to trust God to use them to help effect similar awakenings.

CHAPTER TWO

Here's Life, Asia (Commitment)

Do you not say, "There are yet four months, and then comes the harvest?" Behold, I say to you, lift up your eyes, and look on the fields, that they are white for harvest...

I sent you to reap that for which you have not labored; others have labored, and you have entered into their labor.

John 4:35,38

To develop a strategy that would allow us to saturate large segments of Asia with the gospel was one of my top priorities in 1975 and the subject of much prayer. If we were ever to reach this vast continent with the message of Christ, it would take something unique.

About that time I attended a Here's Life strategy conference in the United States and God began to show me this plan in answer to my prayer. Through Here's Life, the ministry of churches all across Asia could be advanced, and millions of people could be confronted with the claims of Jesus Christ in a very short period of time. I got excited! I realized that God was showing us how a very small number of Christians could expose millions of people to the gospel and giving them an opportunity to receive Christ.

The basic format of Here's Life is to create widespread awareness of the fact that new life can be found in Christ. Many forms of mass media are used to blanket a city aroused, the reveal portion of the campaign declares, "I found it! You can find it, too...new life in Jesus Christ." During this phase, the public is invited to respond by requesting how they can find this new life. Millions of people hear about it, and the thousands who respond are contacted personally by trained campaign workers.

Since 1976, 176,000,000 people in Asia and the Pacific have been exposed to this awareness! Of this figure, more than three million people are known to have indicated positive decisions for Christ. This is staggering to our imaginations, but our Here's Life, Asia records tell us God did indeed work in this way.

The Scripture verses quoted above indicate that frequently we are given the opportunity to reap where we did not sow. Tremendous harvesting is occurring today, but we should remember those who initially planted the fireseeds more than a century ago. Immediately we recall the faithfulness of Carey, Judson, Morris, Taylor and thousands of other missionaries who first carried the gospel message to the nations of this continent. These men and women literally gave their lives and the lives of their husbands, wives and children to take the gospel into untouched areas. Today, more than a century later, we work from the foundation they laid. The Word of God has now been translated into most languages of the world. Small nuclei of believers are located all across Asia, because of the commitment of those early missionaries who dared to "go into all the world."

Thousands of heartwarming – and heartbreaking – stories are told of the zeal, dedication and commitment of the first missionaries and national Christians. These missionaries were committed to reach those to whom God has called them. Details of their stories have been told in other books, but on these pages I want to emphasize that it is they who planted the first fireseeds of the awakening which is taking place today.

As I have criss-crossed the Asian continent during the last decade, I have often asked myself if I would have had the patience or commitment to minister in a country for 16 years without seeing one person come to know Jesus Christ as his personal Lord and Savior. One hundred and fifty years ago, that's exactly what happened in the country of Thailand.

While ministering in the land of Burma (modern-day Thailand), Adoniram Judson translated the entire Bible into Burmese, but it took him 21 years to do it. He also experienced the loss of his wife and several children. Now, a century and a half later, we use his Bible translation in our ministry in Burma every day of the week.

Similar stories of commitment and faithfulness are nestled in the pages of Christian history in Indonesia, Japan, India, China and countries all across this great continent. Because of their endurance and persistence, we are involved in a great spiritual harvest today.

Working with many donominations and organizations, Campus Crusade for Christ International has as its goal to help saturate the entire world with the claims of Jesus Christ. However, even with the great spiritual harvest being experienced today, we still have areas in which we must step out in faith.

Here's Life, India

Consider being faced with the goal of reaching a country of 670 million people with the gospel. This is no easy task. India's population is larger than Africa's and Latin America's combined. Eighty-five percent of the people of India are Hindu, 11% are Muslim and only 2.6% are Christian. These seemingly insurmountable odds baffle us. Add to this the diverse languages spoken and the many cultures represented throughout the 27 states of this country, and obeying the command to "go into all of India" becomes an overwhelming challenge to our human thinking and finite resources.

Yet, much of that nation is being confronted with the claims of Christ today. With modern-day commitment and zeal, Mr. Thomas Abraham, national director of India Campus Crusade for christ and recently-appointed director for Campus Crusade for Christ International's Central Asia and Pacific area of affairs, is leading an unprecedented evangelistic thrust in India.

To date, 101 million people have been confronted with the gospel through his leadership. More than 2.7 million people have indicated decisions to receive Jesus Christ into their lives. Through the combination of the Here's Life campaign, the film, "Jesus," daily evangelistic radio programs and our regular Campus Crusade ministry, unbelievable things are happening in India.

Here's Life, India campaigns have been conducted in 13 major areas, sometimes including entire states of more than 20 million people. These areas include the state of Kerala and the areas of

Bangalore, Vellore, Tirunelveli, Coimbatore, Trichy, Madurai, Madras, Bombay, Hyderabad, Delhi, Balgaum and Dharwar. The total population of these areas includes more than 110 million people. Surveys conducted in each area have revealed that 90% of this incredibly vast population has been made aware of the opportunity to find new life in Christ.

Immediate results of the Here's Life campaign convinced even skeptics of the effectiveness of the movement in helping to spread the gospel throughout India. A pastor from Sawyerpuram in Tirunelveli commented, "Even though I had raised no objections, I doubted that Here's Life, India would work in our Indian villages. I thought it might be successful in Western countries or in big cities where the majority of the people are educated. But, God has now shown me my skepticism was wrong. It works! I have seen responses coming in within the first few hours of the reveal portion of the campaign. God has caused me to change my mind. This will work in India."

In addition to the normal "I found it!" media campaign, the gospel as expressed in the Four Spiritual Laws has been printed in all leading newspapers in these areas. Hundreds of roadside booths have been set up so additional thousands of individuals can hear the gospel message through literature and personal presentations by trained workers. The message of Christ has been presented to millions – literate and illiterate alike.

A church leader exclaimed, "Here's Life stands as one of the greatest strategies ever used in the land of India to develop local churches and help them become Spirit-filled."

Bishop Sam Ponniah of the church of South India in Vellore baptized 11,086 people as a direct result of the Here's Life, Vellore campaign. He says that most of these people are now faithfully attending the churches and in many places new churches are being formed. The vast majority of these who were baptized are from a Hindu background.

Compared with the population, those who have openly indicated decisions for Christ may appear to be a small number. However, taking into account the small percentage of Christians in India and the challenge of the staunch Muslim, Hindu and Buddhist religions which permeate every part of an individual's life, the results are outstanding. Also, we believe there are unknown thousands who have found new life in Christ, but whose conversions have not been reported. Because there are so few churches in so many areas, statistics are scarce.

Examples of God's working abound. In the city of Hyderabad, one of the strongest Muslim areas in all India, a church Bishop reports he baptized 85 people within three weeks of the Here's Life, Hyberabad campaign. Of these, 26 were Muslims.

In South India, Here's Life, Tirunelveli reports indicate that 35,715 people heard the gospel and 7,151 of them placed their trust in Christ. Currently, 305 Bible studies are being conducted for 4,057 of these new believers.

A political leader came to know the Lord through Here's Life, Madras. Later, he and his entire family attended a nearby church where the pastor was speaking on the subject, "Immanuel." Toward the close of the service, he and his family went to the front of the church to ask the pastor to name his 27-day-old child Immanuel. His whole family has accepted the Lord as their Savior and all are growing spiritually.

A highly educated Hindu professor, whose grandfather is a well-known Hindu scholar and interpreter of Hindu scriptures, invited Christ into his life. Immediately, he was forced to leave his home. His peronsal belongings and coveted degree certificates were burned, but his response was, "I will continue to live for Jesus!"

A high official of a southern state (population over 40 million) sent his aide to a neighboring church pastor to request that he come and explain the meaning of "I found it!" The pastor took this opportunity to share with the official how he could find new life in Christ.

As Here's Life volunteers were setting up booths in a local market, Hindu militant groups asked them to leave. Suddenly, a Muslim leader appeared and said, "I have been watching these people for a long time. They are not criticizing our religion. They are talking about Jesus Christ and that is all they are doing. Leave them alone, they have a right to do it." His statement ended the trouble for these workers.

Here's Life, India even touched the secular press. For example, since 45% of the population of Hyderabad is Muslim, our staff members wanted to run "I found it!" advertisements in the Urdu language newspaper owned by Orthodox Muslims. When the advertising manager was approached he said, "We won't print the name of Jesus Christ in our paper." The staff member returned home and prayed about this dilemma. A few days later, he approached the assistant editor who agreed to print the "I found it!" portion of the advertisement, but also insisted that he couldn't publish the Four Spiritual Laws. After giving the advertisement to him, the staff member left, thanking God for this answer to prayer. Following the campaign, the staff member returned to pay for the advertising space and to thank the editor for his cooperation. This Orthodox Muslim replied, "I have not only accepted the advertisement from you, but I have also accepted Jesus Christ as my Lord!"

The "I found it!" phrase made an impact on other groups in India, causing Hindus and Muslims to become afraid of mass conversions. They printed opposing posters with messages such as "I found it in Kashmir," "I found the sweetness of the Hindu religion," and "I found it in Namosivayam." But God used this to create even more curiosity. These opposing posters simply indicated that Christ had become a real issue in this city.

Here's Life, Bangkok – and Jakarta

Here's Life, Bangkok and Here's Life, Jakarta testified that Thai Buddhists and Indonesian Muslims are also hungry to know Christ. During October, 1978, these two capital cities of Asian nations – one predominantly Muslim, the other predominantly Buddhist – rang with the phrase, "I found it!" In each city the small Christian community faced overwhelming obstacles to their efforts to make Christ known, but by faith they proceeded.

In Bangkok, evangelical Christians numbered only a few thousand in a city of more than four million. In this, the capital city of Thailand, the many Buddhist shrines and temples attest to the fact that, for most of the people, "to be a Thai is to be a Buddhist." And in Jakarta, Indonesia, 15% of the 5.5 million people call themselves Christians, but most admit that their indentification is nominal. However, radical anti-Christians have often perpetrated acts of violence against believers.

Supernatural achievements took place in these two cities, even though Here's Life suffered an extreme lack of manpower as well as other major problems. In Bangkok, 13,901 people asked to hear the gospel after seeing mass media messages of "I found it! New life in Jesus Christ." Church workers visited 1,759 inquirers and 6,522 letters were mailed to others.

In Jakarta, meanwhile, 34,531 people responded through the campaign's use of newspapers, radio, posters and literature. Their names were given to church workers who then visited them to relate the gospel. The workers in this Muslim country reported that 966 of the first 1,759 contacted received Christ. Of those, 612 have enrolled in Bible studies. In addition, 27,500 follow-up letters were sent to people who could not be contacted immediately.

The relatively few Here's Life workers in both cities had reason for encouragement through their neighbors' responses. In Jakarta, campaign workers were in awe over the great number of telephone responses. Frequently, another ring sounded the instant a Here's Life phone was returned to its cradle. In Bangkok, hundreds demonstrated hunger for Christ by attaching lengthy letters to response coupons they sent to Here's Life offices.

One man wrote, "I have experienced many problems in my life in both family and work. I have thought to myself that life is useless. I have nothing to depend on. I have heard that Jesus Christ is able to solve man's problems and he can give new life. I am very eager to find this new life and hope that you can help me."

In the predominantly Muslim country of Indonesia, unexpected responses to the media campaign demonstrated a widespread desire to know about Christ. In this country a *hadji* demands respect. He is considered outstanding in his religion, for he has made his *hadj* – a pilgrimage to Mecca. Thus, it must have come as a surprise to Here's Life worker when a middle-aged *hadji* invited him to come and present the gospel.

The *hadji* asked his half-dozen grown children to join him in listening, and soon all were led to receive Christ in prayer. After making arrangements for a later appointment with the Here's Life worker, the respected Muslim man said, "This message should not be for Christians only, but for everyone."

Here's Life, Hong Kong

"A record-breaker in every way," is how one major Hong Kong newspaper described Here's Life, Hong Kong. Trained campaign workers numbered 15,000, while another 85,000 believers took part in other ways. These 100,000 believers – representing about half of the colony's Protestant population – came from 359 participating churches.

Some of the success of this campaign is attributed to the fact that, as the churches began to apply the training in discipleship and evangelism, they experienced a new strength among their members even before the campaign began. Hearing of the other successful campaigns already completed throughout Asia greatly encouraged those Hong Kong churches.

Prior to the March 20-April 5, 1978 media campaign, a missionary guest speaker in a Hong Kong church began his message by endorsing Here's Life, Hong Kong. In response, the pastor tapped the guest on the shoulder and explained that already 70 new members had been added to the church as a result of the outreach by those who had had the Here's Life training. The pastor asked everyone who was present as a result of the training to raise their hands. "Hands went up all over the congregation," recalled the astonished missionary.

During the campaign in Hong Kong, the gospel was presented to 87,174 people, and 28,174 indicated decisions to trust Christ. Of those new Christians, 10,418 enrolled in Bible studies and youth fellowships.

One month later, 200 of the participating churches reported a growth in attendance of betwen 30 and 150 members each. Several congregations have started branch churches.

Before the media campaign began, one pastor decided to test the Here's Life training his congregation had just received. He assembled a team of trained church members, equipped them with witnessing materials and sent them to an island with a population of 1,000 people. The island had no church or evangelsitic activity. Through this effort, 150 of the islanders indicated decisions to trust Christ, and the church established a branch church for these new believers.

In one church of 300 members, 200 had attended the Here's Life training sessions. Skeptical of the program, this pastor also ran a test by sending a team of 50 to a New Territories village where the church had remained a branch church of 15 members for four years. After one month of work by the evangelism team, the church almost tripled in size, with 40 persons in attendance each Sunday. The pastor, now convinced of the training's value, soon began urging others to take advantage of it.

One secular magazine featured a full-color cover article on Here's Life describing "I found it!" as the most successful advertising campaign in the history of Hong Kong. The magazine reported that in 17 days most of the population of Hong Kong had been exposed to this phrase. Our own surveys showed that 85% of the people were aware of "I found it!"

Here's Life, Macau

The tiny Portuguese colony of Macau consists of three small islands off the coast of mainland China, and is probably best known for its casinos. Every weekend tourists pour in from nearby Hong Kong to try their luck in this gambling capital of Asia.

A large group from Hong Kong arrived on August 14, 1978 with quite a different object in mind, however. More than 100 youthful Here's Life, Hong Kong campaign workers and 15 Hong Kong pastors went to Macau to help the colony's small Christian community take the gospel to the 350,000 people of Macau. These young "missionaries" from Hong Kong joined 100 Here's Life, Macau campaign workers. Clad in T-shirts printed with Chinese characters reading, "You must go," they went witnessing door to door throughout Macau in obedience to the Great Commission and with a desire to take new life in Jesus Christ to hundreds waiting to hear this message.

The campaign's first stage consisted of five days of door-to-door witnessing on the major island. Evangelistic meetings were also held each night in the seven churches which participated in the movement. As a result, 6,834 persons heard a presentation of the gospel and 3,258 indicated that they trusted Christ.

One of those seven churches, Lutheran Church Chung Yan Chapel, was, in a sense, really born through Here's Life, Macau. This new chapel had just been established by a missionary and had not really opened for regular services yet, so it had no members. During the first week of the campaign, the chapel saw a particularly good response to its evangelistic meetings, and people from the surrounding area crowded into the chapel for the messages. More than 100 individuals attended the first Sunday service at the new chapel.

Here's Life, Macau differed from other Here's Life movements because all public media, including newspapers, are Communist-controlled and none were available for the media campaign. Therefore, the only things the Christians could use were 15,000 posters and the T-shirts worn by the workers. However, the campaign workers utilized a strategy of sharing the gospel home by home in their effort to saturate the entire colony.

At the end of the first week of follow up, 285 newcomers had attended Sunday church services, 171 individuals had enrolled in Bible studies and 2,710 new believers had been personally visited by campaign workers.

Here's Life, Okinawa

Buddhism and Shintoism are the predominant religions claimed by Okinawa's one million citizens. As a result of Here's Life, Okinawa, the Christian population of this Japanese island has increased significantly and is still growing. Approximately one third of Okinawa's Christian population of 3,000 took active roles in the media campaign, which saw 1,147 Okinawans indicate decisions to receive Christ as Savior. These 1,000 Christian workers were from 57 of the island's approximately 100 churches.

More than 300 prayer groups were formed to pray for the campaign. One answer to prayer concerned the media. Posters and small cloth billboards are common forms of advertising in Okinawa, and periodically the city government removes them. The morning the "I found it!" posters and billboards were displayed, a campaign worker heard that the city had chosen that morning for one of these periodic cleanups. Workers at the "I found it!" telephone center prayed that the campaign posters and billboards would remain untouched. Amazingly, after the city government workers finished the cleanup, all advertising was gone except the "I found it!" posters – making the campaign even more visible.

During the months leading up to the campaign, some churches gave the Here's Life 20-hour course in discipleship and evangelism as many as 25 times. Thoroughness and flexibility in the instruction was possible because of the use of mediated training units. One pastor, seeing the lights of his church on at night, discovered his laymen training each other with the mediated unit.

In all, more than 800 church members completed the entire course. Before the media campaign began, 428 people indicated they received Christ when these trained believers shared the gospel with them.

In addition to conducting thorough pre-campaign training, the churches established 468 Bible study groups in advance of the campaign. These were formed in order to insure that people who received Christ during the campaign would have a continuing opportunity to grow in their faith.

Here's Life Means Changed Lives

There are many exciting stories of how lives were changed during the Here's Life campaigns as Jesus Christ was lifted up before the lost people of the world by committed Christian workers across Asia. To conclude this chapter, I want to relate three of these. One story concerns a Buddhist, another a Hindu and the third a Muslim.

In Bangkok, Thailand, a Buddhist teenage girl was tired of life as she was experiencing it. Deciding to end it all, she climbed out on a window ledge of her fourth-story apartment, planning to leap to the pavement below. Perching on the edge, she noticed a sign on the street below. It was well lighted and clearly visible from her angle. The sign said, "I found it! You can find it too. New life in Jesus Christ." A telephone number was listed on the sign. The young lady studied the sign for a moment and decided she had absolutely nothing to lose by trying this number. With this ray of hope, she climbed back through the window, returned to her apartment, and made the call. A campaign worker came to visit her. Through the presentation of the gospel message she found hope and new meaning for her life. She now is very active in a Bangkok church.

In India, a Brahmin Hindu became frustrated with his life and decided to go to a certain place and commit suicide. On his way, he saw a Here's Life poster which proclaimed, "I found it! You can find it too. New life in Jesus Christ." He began thinking, vaguely impressed that the message might contain an answer to his desperation. Finally, he decided he would try Jesus Christ before committing suicide. He wrote a letter to the Here's Life office and, as a result, a campaign worker contacted him and explained to him the lasting solution to his intense frustration. With tears rolling down his face, he received Christ. This Brahmin Hindu dramatically found new life.

The story regarding the Muslim is somewhat different. In Indonesia a young man responded to the Here's Life campaign, and a Campus Crusade for Christ staff member called at his home to share Christ with him. The father of the young inquirer was a devout Muslim. Very politely, the father offered the staff member a cup of tea and with it, poisoned him.

For several days our staff member was at the point of death, but God spared his life. Upon leaving the hospital, he returned to the home of the man who had poisoned him. There he expressed his love for him and assured the man of God's love.

The man could not refuse this love and, as a result, a Bible study is now being conducted in his home. To date, he has not accepted Christ as his Savior, but we are confident that as he continues to study, God's Word will accomplish the purpose for which God sent it.

God honors faithfulness and commitment. When His children believe Him, He does the impossible. I am convinced that the stories told in these pages would not have occurred had it not been for the dedication and obedience of committed men and women through the ages who have invested their lives to help change the world.

Fireseeds of this awakening were planted decades ago by committed individuals. They continue to be planted today on an even larger scale by thousands more who want to help reap the most abundant spiritual harvest Christian history has ever known. The gospel fire is spreading and millions are coming to know the Lord.

CHAPTER THREE

Greater Works Than These Shall You Do (Power)

Truly, truly, I say to you, he who believes in Me, the works that I do shall he do also; and greater works than these shall he do; because I go to the Father. And whatever you ask in My name, that will I do, that the Father may be glorified in the Son. If you ask Me anything in My name, I will do it...

And I will ask the Father, and He will give you another Helper, that He may be with you forever.

John 14:12-14,16

As difficult as it is for us to understand and believe, we who know Christ personally and walk in His power can do greater works than Jesus Christ Himself did. This is possible when we are involved in the worldwide sharing of the gospel. Multitudes can be added to the body of Christ daily of the indwelling power of the Holy Spirit in the life of each believer.

In 1980 an estimated 11 million Asians, Micronesians, Melanesians and Polynesians indicated personal decisions for Christ. Our staff members, working with Christians of many denominations and organizations, had shared the gospel through such exciting strategies as Here's Life, Asia, including the film, "Jesus," which depicts Christ's life and ministry, radio programs, campus ministries, and village outreaches. Now, people are still being evangelized, and as discipleship takes place, existing churches are growing and new churches are springing up.

This is just the beginning of great things and in 1981 we are sure, even greater results will be experienced. Yet, if men were attempting to do these things in their own strength, their efforts would be futile. I believe the key to the phenomenal things that are taking place today is found in three promises made by Christ:

Promise 1: "Greater works than these shall he do; because I go to the Father."

Promise 2: "Whatever you ask in My name, that will I do."

Promise 3: "He will give you another Helper."

There seems to be more discussion about the ministry of the Holy Spirit today than in the past decades. I am thankful for this, yet there still seems to be a need for further explanation concerning this indwelling power which is ours. Many Christians do not know how to walk day by day in the power of the Holy Spirit.

Dr. Bill Bright often shares this example when introducing his message on how to be filled with the Holy Spirit:

"Some years ago, at one of our Lay Institutes for Evangelism in Seattle, Washington, attended by more than 4,000 trainees, I gave a message on how to be filled with the Holy Spirit. Afterward, a missionary who had just retired after 20 years of service in Africa came to see me. He was very excited as he came to share how, during that meeting, he had finally found what he had sought throughout his entire Christian life.

"'Today, as you spoke,' he said, 'I was filled with the Spirit. For 20 years I have tried to serve God on the mission field, but I have served Him in the energy of the flesh and have had very few results. Now, though I have retired and returned to America, I want to go back to Africa.

"'This time, I want to concentrate on working just with missionaries, because I know from experience that many of them are still searching for what I have sought all these years. The most important message I can take to them is how they can be filled with the Holy Spirit by faith.

"'I want to teach them what you taught me so that they, in turn, will be able to teach the Africans how they too can be filled with the Spirit.'"

This example typifies many believers. They do not know that one is filled with the Holy Spirit by faith.

We *receive Christ* by faith: "For by grace you have been saved through faith; and that not of yourselves, it is the gift of God; not as a result of works, that no one should boast" (Ephesians 2:8,9).

We *walk* by faith: "As you therefore have received Christ Jesus the Lord, so walk in Him" (Colossians 2:6).

We are *filled with the Holy Spirit* by faith. In Scripture we find a command and a promise which tell us that we can claim the fullness of the Holy Spirit by faith. The command: Be filled with the Spirit. "And do not get drunk with wine, for that is dissipation, but be filled with the Spirit" (Ephesians 5:18). The promise: He will always answer when we pray according to His will. "And this is the confidence which we have before Him, that, if we ask anything according to His will, He hears us. And if we know that He hears us in whatever we ask, we know that we have the requests which we have asked from Him" (I John 5:14,15).

In Fiji recently, one of our staff members conducted a training session in which he explained how to be filled with the Holy Spirit by faith. A pastor who had taken the training commented, "I am 78 years old and I have been preaching for over 50 years. Today, I discovered how to be filled with the Holy Spirit. Now I understand the power and resources available to me and I can freely cast my cares on the Lord."

A student in Korea said, "It was through the training that I learned how I can live by faith in the power of the Holy Spirit. I have been a Christian for some time, and I prayed regularly, but still I was so weak. Now I know He gives me strength and I share Christ wherever I go—on buses, at school and at home. My family has become Christian and we are so happy together. God gives me power to live for Him through the Holy Spirit."

Without this indwelling power we are weak, but as we experience the power, even greater things than those we ask God to do through us will take place. This power goes far beyond anything for which we can believe Him. The Apostle Paul said it best: "Now glory be to God who by His mighty power at work within us is able to do far more than we would ever dare to ask or even dream of—infinitely beyond our highest prayers, desires, thoughts, or hopes. May He be given glory forever and ever through endless ages because of His master plan of salvation for the church through Jesus Christ" (Ephesians 3:20,21 TLB).

His Mighty Power Exceeds Man's Plans

A situation took place in Burma two years ago which is now resulting in hundreds of thousands of Burmese being confronted with the claims of Christ. A group of our Burma staff members began to plan for the fulfillment of the Great Commission in their country. This was an extremely optimistic vision when you consider that Burma is a closed socialistic country where Buddhism is the state religion. A solid Christian foundation existed within the church, but very little was happening outside. Evangelistic meetings were conducted in churches from time to time, but little was being done to appeal to the masses. The staff members asked God to empower them and to give them His wisdom as they planned what seemed to be an unattainable goal.

They knew from the contacts made in their daily ministries that Buddhists are open and responsive to the gospel. Because of this they decided to hold large outdoor evangelistic meetings. Church leaders were contacted regarding their support and participation. These leaders were not enthusiastic and felt that outdoor meetings would not be successful. The staff members asked the leaders why this could not be done. The only reason given was that it had never been done before.

Trusting the Lord to do great things, the staff members began on a small scale with a few outdoor evangelistic meetings in the city of Rangoon. God honored their faith and obedience. Soon people began to attend by the thousands. During 1980, more than 134,000 people heard the gospel in these open air meetings and follow-up literature was given to all who desired it. An additional 176,000 Burmese saw the "Jesus" film during the last three months of 1980. Thus far, film teams have experienced no serious opposition to their meetings. All of this happened because a small group of Spirit-filled Christians believed God's promises and began acting upon them.

The Holy Spirit Prepares Hearts

The Holy Spirit not only opens doors, as in Burma, but He also prepares the hearts of people to receive His message.

For several years a Japanese student had been wondering if there was a purpose for his life. Not being a very outgoing person, he had difficulty making friends and spent most of his time alone. When members of a religious cult approached him on his university campus, he was interested. They seemed to offer friendship and hope for the future which he had been unable to find. He attended their meetings, but gradually became disillusioned with their teaching. After four months, he quit because this had not met his need.

About a month later in the gymnasium of his university, he found a brochure advertising the Nagoya Billy Graham Crusade. These brochures were being distributed by Japan Campus Crusade for Christ. Although he was helping to finance his college education by delivering newspapers each afternoon, he took an afternoon off to attend the Billy Graham Crusade, hoping to find what he was searching for. He also completed the response card in the brochure and mailed it to the Campus Crusade office in Nagoya. Soon a staff member contacted this spiritually hungry student and set up an appointment with him. Together they read through the gospel as presented in the Four Spiritual Laws and the student prayed and received Christ.

This student continues to meet weekly with our staff member in preparation for an outreach on his campus. He also joined a church near his home and is meeting individually with the pastor each week.

When asked how his life had changed since receiving Christ, he replied, "Before coming to know God, I didn't understand the purpose of life. But now I want everyone to have the joy of knowing Jesus."

Traveling and searching for truth and happiness occupied 23 years in the life of one elderly woman in northeast Thailand. Recently she dreamed that she entered the spirit world where the dead dwell. In her dream she saw sad, ghost-like creatures in cramped, gloomy quarters. A sign above these quarters said, "This is where the Buddhists go." A little farther on she heard music and singing. She saw people who were happy and comfortable. The sign above that door said, "This is where people who believe in Jesus Christ go." Upon awakening she expressed her desire to become a Christian and immediately invited Christ into her life. Her son, who had often told her about Christ and prayed for her, was overjoyed with the way in which the Holy Spirit had worked in her heart.

The Holy Spirit Schedules Divine Appointments

While in Hawaii on his way to the island of Guam, one of our American staff members visited a large shopping center. When he began a conversation with a sailor, he planned to share Christ with him. However, the sailor had to leave before he had the opportunity to do so. He began praying that someone would share the gospel with this sailor.

Several months later, the staff member was jogging in Guam. He suddenly recognized the same sailor and stopped to talk with him. The sailor was scheduled to be on board a ship somewhere in the South Pacific, but the ship was in need of repair and had stopped in Guam for two days until the repairs could be made. The staff member took advantage of this second opportunity, and shared the gospel as contained in the Four Spiritual Laws with the sailor. Upon hearing the message of God's love and forgiveness, the sailor invited Christ into his life.

The Holy Spirit Protects

God's hand of protection has been on the many hundreds of Campus Crusade staff members and volunteers working across Asia. In spite of the fact that a number of them minister in remote and dangerous areas, no one has been killed or seriously injured.

An example of God's protective care occurred when one of our teams in India was delayed by a police inspector for several days on a trip to a certain village. At the exact time they would have been in the village, it was destroyed by a flood.

Another incident happened in Bangladesh, where two campus staff men were working in the city of Norshindi. Several times as they were sharing their faith on a college campus, the students became angry and threatened them. On different occasions, the men were even driven off the campus. However, they both returned and continued to share the gospel. One day, 2,000 people gathered around them and began to beat them attempting to pull out the eyes of one. The two men said they were not trying to force anyone to become a Christian – they were just following the Lord's command to tell people about Jesus. The crowd told them they must leave or they would be killed, so finally the two young men were forced to return to Dacca.

Another Bangladesh staff man was sharing his faith in an Urdu camp when he was severely beaten. But he continues his ministry. "This persecution is a very, very common thing in our country, a Muslim state," said Bangladesh's national director.

In Nepal Christians are constantly threatened with imprisonment, and they face the dangers of traveling on rough, steep mountain trails. In the Philippines, staff members have been stoned, and at least once, a hand grenade was thrown into the crowd at a film showing. Instead of giving up, these hardships seem to cause Asian Christians to be even more determined to communicate the gospel.

Our Own Sphere of Influence

The Holy Spirit desires to use each of us in our sphere of influence. Is it your desire to see an awakening take place in your area? Do you have a burden for revival in your nation and the world? Civilization is without hope unless God intervenes with His supernatural power. Christians must appropriate this power. This awakening in Asia will continue only so long as Christians boldly move to the front line of the spiritual battle in evangelism and discipleship.

I personally believe that this awakening *will* continue. This fire will spread and grow, day by day – even in places where we least expect it – when Christians appropriate the power of the Holy Spirit.

For example, a fireseed is spreading even in a miserable disease-infested refugee camp.

Khao I Dong is the largest Cambodian refugee camp in Thailand. I visited this camp which is located only a few kilometers from the Thai-Kampuchea (Cambodian) border. My purpose for going was two-fold.

First, I wanted to visit the 70-year-old father of Taing Vek Huong, our Cambodian staff member who miraculously escaped Kampuchea one year before. Huong and his wife, Samoeun, also at least 34 other relatives in the camp. They were friends whom I had not seen for more than five years. What a joy it was to see them again, even in these conditions.

Second, I went to see for myself the tragic situation which had captured the attention of the world. I wanted to explore possibilities for a spiritual ministry for our staff and ways we could help meet needs there.

What I saw cannot be described verbally – only experienced! One hundred and thirteen thousand people were situated in temporary bamboo housing – which may become very permanent.

The Thai government, the United Nations and many secular and Christian relief organizations are doing much to meet the needs of those people, but still the needs are overwhelming. I am accustomed to traveling in rough places, but seldom have I seen conditions like those. For one thing, as I sat down to talk with friends, hundreds of flies settled on me. This fact alone can enable you to imagine what other conditions existed in that camp.

However, in spite of that deplorable situation, God is at work in an unusual way. While standing in the recently-built Khao I Dong church, which was a truly beautiful bamboo and thatch structure seating 700 on bamboo benches, I talked with the brother and brother-in-law of our staff member.

"How many Cambodian Christians are estimated to be here in the camp now?" I asked. Their immediate reply was "More than 20,000." I was speechless. That is almost seven times more Christians than there were in the entire country of Cambodia when it fell to the Khmer Rouge on April 17, 1975.

To see the commitment of these young Christians filled me with joy. They witness daily in teams and Bible studies meet each day all across the camp. Believers fill the church each morning from 7:30 to 8:30 for prayer time. The Spirit of God is moving across that camp in a wonderful way. I was told that the church is packed and 6,000 people crowd outside each week for Sunday services. Fortunately, the church has an excellent loud-speaker system and there are no side walls, so the people who have gathered outside can also participate in the service.

I had the thrilling opportunity of addressing one of the many Bible study groups. Forty-eight people were packed into the living quarters of a family of ten. The space we occupied was about 8 feet wide and 16 feet long. I asked the group, "How many of you were Christians before you left Cambodia?" Not one hand was raised. All 48 had received Jesus Christ as their Savior during the few short months since they had arrived in Khao I Dong. Later, I learned this was true of most of the 20,000 Christians in the camp.

As I looked at this group, I sensed that the months of hunger they had endured, the deaths they had witnessed and the heartache they had experienced was worth it because they had met Jesus Christ. They realized He alone could solve their problems. He alone could give them peace. These Christians have nothing but Jesus, and they are happy.

Emotions overcame me as we drove out of the gates of Khao I Dong and began the four-hour trip back to Bangkok. Never have

I been so in awe of the sovereignty of God. The Cambodian people are enduring more tragedy than most of us will hear about in a lifetime. But this is bringing many of them to the foot of the cross where they are finding the permanent solution to their spiritual needs.

As we drove along, my mind raced back to my first trip to Cambodia in the spring of 1972. At that time, there were reported to be 300 Christians in the entire nation. When the nation fell in April, 1975, the estimate was 3,000.

Now, five years later, I have been told there were 20,000 Christians in one refugee camp. My heart sang praises as I lifted my eyes from their catastrophe and realized what God had done among the Cambodian people.

The results can be overwhelming when we allow the Holy Spirit to empower us and use us in our spheres of influence. Khao I Dong is the ultimate example of what the Holy Spirit will do when a believer yields his life to Him. The original handful of Kampuchean Christians in this camp had nothing going for them from a human standpoint. They had just endured five years of total deprivation and were now delivered into a steaming jungle of misery – but they still believed Jesus could use them.

Christ's promises hold true. In Khao I Dong, India, Japan, Europe, Africa or America, He uses Spirit-filled people. Remember those great promises?

"Greater works than these shall he do because I go to the Father." "Whatever you ask in my name, that will I do." "The Father will give you another Helper."

The Spirit-filled life is the Christ-controlled life by which Christ lives His life in and through us in the power of the Holy Spirit. We are filled with the Holy Spirit by faith. As we sincerely desire His control and empowering, and by faith claim His fulness, we will become fireseeds – flames used to awaken our world to the marvelous message of God's love.

PART II
Awakening

CHAPTER FOUR

Jesus Speaks Bengali

"Son, Jesus speaks Bengali," stated an intriguing letter sent to a Bangladesh pastor, who was in the United States taking advanced theological studies for his doctorate degree. The letter had been written by his saintly mother who had seen the film "Jesus," in her native Bengali tongue the previous evening in her village. Not fully aware of the wonders of our technical age, she was overcome with the fact that she had seen Jesus speak her own language during the film. Her son explained to me that, in her thinking, she literally saw her Lord before her own eyes.

Even though I am accustomed to working with village people whose lifestyle is very simple, the statement "Jesus speaks Bengali" is difficult for me to understand, as it may be for many. However, similar statements arrive in our office regularly, telling of the delight experienced by village people as they hear "Jesus speak" in their own language.

For more than a decade Campus Crusade has prayed that Asia would be reached for Christ by 1980. Here's Life, Asia was sent by the Lord to expose many millions of people in the large cities to the gospel; yet 80% of the continent lives in a rural setting.

God again proved His timing is perfect. When our need to expand to the rural areas was greatest, He sent us the film "Jesus." Campus Crusade for Christ has the rights to this film in all Asian countries and the Pacific Islands.

"Jesus," which took nine years of preparation and involved a cast of 5,000, presents an authentic, accurate re-enactment of

Luke's account of the life of our Lord. The film's historical accuracy has been checked and rechecked by 200 biblical scholars. And, with more than 30 previous films already produced on the life of Christ, this is the first to be filmed entirely in the Holy Land. Scenes were filmed on or very near the actual locations where the events took place. The film also accurately presents Christ's miracles and concludes with His ascension into heaven.

In "Jesus," the emphasis is on Christ – who speaks only His own words from Scripture and, for that reason, dialogue other than that found in Luke's Gospel is kept to a minimum.

When you see Christ in this film, you can believe that He spent 18 years in a carpenter's shop before He started His ministry. None of the reverence and respect have been sacrificed, but the portrayal is of a strong and muscular man. He can smile and laugh and share His emotions with people.

Films have long been a popular form of entertainment in Asia. They are a guaranteed crowd-gatherer whether shown in a movie theater, a community park, a village square, or on a street corner. In China, for example, 480 million people attend films each week. On an average, teenagers there see them every other day. People begin standing in line as early as 5 a.m. in order to attend the first showing at 5:30 a.m.

In India 75% of the population lives in rural areas. Films shown in this country attract cumulative audiences of more than three billion people annually.

"Jesus" in 30 Languages

The film, "Jesus," has been translated into 30 languages of Asia and the Pacific. This is a first in the history of the film industry, including all Christian and secular films. I am told if a film is a success in the western world, it is usually sub-titled in an average of five other languages. And usually the language is not changed through lip-synchronization. When professional filmmakers heard our plans to lip-sync 22 languages in four months, they informed us that this was not possible.

However, they did not realize that the Lord has promised to do the impossible. In four months, 22 languages were reproduced! This becomes even more of a miracle when you realize that some Asian languages, such as Thai, require twice the length of time to say the same thing as in English. More than

800 prints have been distributed in 32 Asian countries. These 30 languages represent a potential audience of 1.5 billion people.

This film has proven invaluable in communicating the gospel. During 1980, 500 rural film teams traveled with it in India, the Philippines, Korea, Indonesia, Thailand, Bangladesh, Sri Lanka, Burma, Nepal, Malaysia, and the islands of Micronesia, Melanesia, and Polynesia. This strategy will continue into the eighties. India alone will have 200 films teams to cover that massive area.

In India, each two-man team travels from village to village carrying with them a power generator, a projector and a collapsible screen. Using telescoping aluminum tubing, the men can erect a giant frame for the screen, set up the projector and generator, and within a few minutes thousands of people hear the words of Jesus which have been dubbed in their local dialect. The film concludes with a short summary of the gospel and an invitation to receive Christ so that millions upon millions of people throughout Asia can clearly hear how to respond to the Savior they have seen represented on the screen.

In Fiji, it is said that the first book ever written in the Fijian language was the Bible. It is now being said that the first film ever produced in the Fijian language is "Jesus." The same claim can be made for many of these 30 languages.

It has been an exciting privilege for us to be able to present the message of Christ to hundreds of millions of people who, for the first time, are hearing the gospel. For many of them, it is also the first time they have viewed a motion picture.

We Christians know there is nothing more powerful than the gospel message. When people have the opportunity to hear what this message involves, I believe most will respond positively and receive Christ into their lives. The tragedy is that most people in rural areas have never had the opportunity to hear this wonderful message of God's love. Through strategies such as using this film, however, this situation is changing.

"Jesus" Opens Doors

In Indonesia, the largest Muslim country in the world, "Jesus" was shown to 218,000 people in November and December of 1980. It is estimated that at least 50% of those who saw the film were Muslims. According to the laws of that land, it is prohibited for such a film as "Jesus" to be shown outside a church building because this is considered forcing Christianity on the non-Christian population. The film is easily being shown inside churches but this does not reach the non-Christian majority. Therefore, our staff members have boldly approached leaders of Muslin villages and explained the use of the film to them. When they ask permission to show the film in the village, very few leaders say no. With permission granted, it then becomes legal for an outdoor showing. Through this strategy of directly approaching village leaders, hundreds of thousands of Muslims are hearing the gospel, many for the first time.

In the Indonesian village of Polobogo, situated 7 miles southwest of Salatiga, 99% of the population are nominal Muslims. With special permission of the village leader, our staff members were able to show "Jesus." As they finished the third reel and were preparing to show the fourth and final reel, the village chief requested an opportunity to speak to the audience. He surprised everyone by saying, "Ladies and gentlemen, as you enjoy this film, I hope you will seriously consider its message. This is a repentance film, presenting Jesus Christ who died to redeem us from the power of our sins. He came to offer salvation to us. Therefore, people of Polobogo, though you already profess a religion, you never practice it, so I encourage you to change your religion to Christianity. The Christian religion is admitted and legal. Do not be hesitant or be afraid to accept it. Tonight you may begin to consider it and whenever you decide to accept Christianity, please contact these people or the nearest local church."

Subsequent to this showing, and the surprise announcement, last December the village chief and his family accepted Christ, and some of the villagers followed his step of faith. For the first time, this village chief celebrated Christmas in his home.

In Malaysia, the language groups of the people are intermingled, unlike many countries where a different language is spoken in each state. In Malaysia it is possible to go into an area where five languages are spoken, usually two Chinese languages, Bahasa Malay, an Indian language and English. It is an extensive undertaking to have sufficient films to enable the teams to reach the major language groups in these areas.

In Sarawak, East Malaysia, the staff visited a village which is believed to have one of the largest "long houses" in the country. A long house is as its name describes – a very long house. Rather than living in small detached dwellings, many families live under one roof. For each additional family they simply add another "house" to the end of the building and it becomes longer and longer. This long house had 120 doors and each door represented one family.

"Jesus" was shown for 2,000 people in the village basketball court located beside this long house. Although it began to rain, the people remained in their places. Following the movie, the village people entertained our team with local folk dances and songs. To reach the village the team had had to travel by boat for two hours and then they walked for six hours, climbing up the mountain carrying their equipment. Needless to say, they were tired! However, after the entertainment by the villagers, the village chief asked that the movie be shown once more. They finished the second showing at 3 a.m.

Each time the crucifixion scene appeared on the screen, these 2,000 villagers began to cry aloud. It is estimated that over 25% of those who saw the movie prayed to receive Christ into their lives.

In another Malaysian village, our staff showed the film to 300 people. During the session at the conclusion of the film, 30 people raised their hands indicating that they had received Christ. Among those 30 people was the chief of that village. The chief was not satisfied that out of 300 people, only 30 had responded. Again, our staff members were greatly surprised when he said, "I command every one of you to pray to receive Christ, and raise up your hands!" Everyone raised his hand. All the people changed their religion by the command of their chief.

As strange as it may seem, this is not an unusual occurrence. Certainly, most of these people have not been born-again, and they are not included in our statistics. However, by merely changing their religion, they are now open to the teachings of Christ. Throughout the jungles of east Malaysia and Indonesia today, many genuine Christian villages have resulted from a mass-conversion decision made on the part of the chief.

During October, November and December, 1980, India was filled with violence, riots, floods and bad weather of all kinds, yet 3.9 million people saw "Jesus." At that time 70 of our projected 200 film teams were operating. The stories relating to these initial several million who heard the gospel give us a foretaste of the exciting events that are before us when the remainder of our India film teams go into operation in 1981.

In a village in the state of Karnataka, a gospel team desired to conduct an open-air meeting. The villagers objected and threatened them by saying they would burn their van and their gospel tracts. Regretfully, the team had to leave the village without holding the meeting. The next day one of our film teams arrived in the village. They discussed showing the film with the leaders and the leaders agreed to arrange it. To the amazement of our film team, more than 5,000 people rushed to view the film. Not one objection was raised. Instead they requested we also show the film in nearby areas.

In another village the only possibility for getting electricity to operate the projector was from the Hindu temple. This was a Hanuman (monkey god) temple with only one electrical outlet – a light bulb which burned day and night in the forehead of the monkey god! Although this light normally was never turned off, the temple authorities willingly removed the bulb from the monkey's head and allowed us to use that place to connect with the electricity. Thus, the people of that village heard the message of Christ as they saw the film, "Jesus."

In Maharashtra state, 24 people in one village came forward requesting baptism after one film showing. In another village, most of the people invited Jesus Christ into their lives after the village chief publicly professed he had received Him into his life.

Needless to say, many unique things have happened as "Jesus" has been shown across India. Electrical failures during showings are commonplace. However, people remain seated, patiently waiting for the supply of electricity to return so they can see the entire movie. Several times, showings beginning in the evening were concluded at 5:30 the next morning after the electricity returned around 3 a.m.

There is a tremendous eagerness in the hearts of these rural people to watch the life of our Lord. In one place, when the electricity failed, some of the Hindu leaders came forward and challenged the strength of our God. The staff prayed and, to the astonishment of the Hindu leaders, the Lord answered and the electric power was restored.

In another area, the authorities in charge of a Hindu festival asked our staff if the film could be shown on the final day of their festival. More than 10,000 people came for this showing. The movie theater nearby canceled their regular showing because no one was in the theater.

In the same state, a large Christian crusade was being conducted. They requested our staff to show "Jesus" to the 20,000 people who were gathered. According to crusade officials, at least 10,000 of them indicated they had invited Christ into their lives at the conclusion of the film.

Traditionally, Hindus worship many gods. However, in spite of the emphasis given in the film that Christ is the only way and the only Savior, many Hindu villagers are asking if we can show the film in their areas. Thousands of them are accepting Christ into their lives as their only Savior. It is estimated that an average of 30% of all those who see the film in India are committing their lives to Christ.

"Jesus" Filmstrip Widely Used

Still photos taken during the motion picture filming of "Jesus" have been used to develop an invaluable tool – a 30-minute "Jesus" filmstrip. For millions of people throughout Asia and the Pacific, seeing this filmstrip will be their first clear exposure to the gospel.

The object of the filmstrip is to show in a more abbreviated form, who Jesus Christ is and how to begin a personal relationship with Him. This important tool is also used for follow-up to reinforce the message presented through the movie.

The 154-slide filmstrip, with an English soundtrack, has also been translated into more than 30 major Asian and Pacific languages. Approximately 5,500 filmstrips have been produced and distributed along with mediated training units already in use in Campus Crusade ministries throughout Asia.

Because minimal equipment is needed to show the filmstrip, presentations can easily be made in a variety of settings: inside or outside, in homes, community buildings, churches or classrooms. The lightweight equipment can be powered by available electricity, batteries or a generator.

In many areas of Papua New Guinea, for example, the population is spread across the country in small clusters. The filmstrip is being used very effectively to reach these groups of people who have had little exposure to the gospel.

Follow-up of Millions

How to follow up and instruct the millions who respond to the gospel message as a result of seeing "Jesus" has been one of our greatest challenges. The procedures vary from country to country.

If there is a local church in the area, the film teams work directly with the church and all who see the film are encouraged to attend the church. However, whether there is a local church or not, initial follow-up is conducted on the spot by the film team. At the conclusion of the film a copy of the Four Spiritual Laws booklet is presented to each person attending. Then, a meeting is announced for the next evening.

The next day the film team moves on to another village while a follow-up team remains in the first village to conduct the evening meeting. The filmstrip is shown, which reinforces what was seen the previous night and helps give assurance of salvation. Initial follow-up materials are presented and explained, three booklets, which cover assurance of salvation, basic Christian growth and how to study the Bible, along with the gospel of Luke. Then everyone is also encouraged to listen to the local Here's Life radio program which will give them further follow-up and daily discipleship training.

Modern-day circuit riders have been thoroughly trained and have been given a prescribed number of villages to visit. They report to their supervisors weekly. You can imagine the tons of literature required to implement this strategy alone. Last year, for instance, 15,000,000 copies of the Four Spiritual Laws booklet were printed and distributed across India.

Team Logistics Planned

Maintenance of records showing the areas covered by each team and planning where they should go next has also been an extensive undertaking. Let's continue using India as our example. This is the second-most populous country in the world, with 670 million people. In my opinion, if India can be saturated we should be able to reach any country in the world.

As the India staff met to contemplate their strategy, it was determined from past experience that a film showing could draw viewers from an area of nine square kilometers. This is not too far for people to walk at night, and an effective publicity campaign can be carried out in a few hours. With this in mind, large maps of

India were divided into 31,200 sections, each representing one nine-kilometer square, and each square has been numbered.

As weekly reports come into the national headquarters, we can determine exactly where each team has been.

Next, the complicated organizational structure for distributing films and equipment was set up. This planning includes projectors, speakers, mediated training units and microphones, plus record-keeping and supervision of the distribution.

Our prayer target is for each of the 200 film teams across India to cover one nine-kilometer square per day. If they are able to do this, the film will be made available to 96% of India's population within a six-month period. The minimum audience size in India is estimated to be 3,000 people. If each team covers one section per day, in six months we will have shown the film to at least 120 million people in India.

"Jesus" Appeals to All Segments of Society

One of the unique features of this film is its appeal to all segments of society. An India state governor, a large metropolitan city mayor, the prime-minister of a nation and villagers on small remote islands in the Pacific have all responded positively to its message. The power of the gospel transcends all cultural, economic, racial and religious barriers.

Even the Punjab area of North India, which is the stronghold of the Sikh people, has been awakened to the gospel through the use of this film. The Christian population there is almost nil. However, the Lord has performed many life-changing miracles through several leaders of the Sikh religion. After seeing the film, one of these leaders, who has earned a double master's degree from a university, said, "Before, I knew very little about Christianity and the teachings of Christ, but now I realize that Jesus is the only answer." He asked to be baptized immediately. When a new believer from an eastern religion is baptized, he must seriously consider the cost. Often he is turning his back on everything he had previously valued, and is in effect giving up his family and friends for the sake of the gospel.

When "Jesus" was shown in India's Karnataka state Officers Club, the Hindu secretary of the club said, "This club has been in existence for 20 years but we have never had a religious program before. However, this film on the life of Christ has had an impact in the lives of the people here."

The film was even shown in a governor's palace in India. The governor, his entire family and 125 guests attended and heard the gospel.

A pastor on one of the Solomon Islands reported that he had been baptized and had followed the teaching of his church all his life, so he felt that he was a Christian. However, after he saw the film and read the booklet, "How to be Sure You are a Christian," he realized his need for a personal Savior. As a result, he invited Christ into his life.

A common tendency of Christians is to ask God to perform miracles, and then, when He does, experience amazement. Bangladesh is a place where God is heaping one miracle on top of another, and I, for one, continue to be amazed. In the last six months of 1980, 491,115 people saw "Jesus." The majority of these were Hindu, and animal-worshipping, tribal people. It is estimated that more than 255,000 of this number have indicated positive decisions for Christ.

In the Chittagong area of Bangladesh, the military brigadier and his staff viewed the film. Becoming enthusiastic, the brigadier said, "All the people of this area should see this film!" His excitement carried over into action as he used government vehicles to transport the film crews and their equipment from village to village.

In addition to its rural influence, the film is being used effectively in large metropolitan cities across Asia. In order to continuously saturate Singapore with the gospel, a commercial venture was undertaken. Most of the churches in the country cooperated in renting one of the most popular theaters in Singapore for eight weeks, from March 12 through June 10, 1981. A massive media advertising campaign was conducted to attract an anticipated 450,000 people. This means that one-fifth of Singapore's 2.2 million population was directly exposed to the gospel during the eight weeks the film was shown. A similar strategy is taking place in three major Malaysian cities.

An exciting aspect for all the film teams is the way they are supported by local people. In country after country, local government officials, Christians and even non-Christians feed the teams, offer transportation and donate gasoline for the generators.

"Jesus" Clears Customs

Another miracle relating to "Jesus" involves the customs charges and the clearance of the film and the equipment in the various countries. The Lord has enabled us to save hundreds of thousands of dollars in customs charges, and we have been able to get the film into Muslim countries where the laws of that country normally forbid importing a Christian film.

Bangladesh is just one beautiful example of how the Lord worked on our behalf when our staff attempted to clear the film prints into that country. The following story, related by our Bangladesh director, gives the details of one of God's miracles:

"It was very difficult to obtain the import permit. When I first met the Controller of Import and Export, he asked why we wanted to import 20 films and projectors. I replied, 'For religious purposes.' He asked, 'Why then are these films in Bengali rather than English?' adding his concern that if the film is widely shown we will misguide the Muslims. His decision was that he could not give permission to issue an import permit.

"As I returned to my office, I was perplexed regarding the next step I should take. My staff began praying earnestly about this situation. We also asked churches to pray and we began a 24-hour prayer chain.

"A few days later, one of my friends came to visit and said he had heard we were having a problem with the film. He offered to help us since he is a very close friend of the Controller. When we met with the Controller, my friend explained that I am his friend and he should issue the import permit for the films.

"After a long discussion, the Muslim Controller said, 'I will give you the permit, but you must still obtain the approval of the censor board.'

"We found the secretary of the censor board to be very helpful. He told us to return within a week and we would have the approval. A week later, he said, 'I am sorry, but I cannot give you the film. The members of the censor board who have seen it feel that the entire board should see it because it is such a serious film.' The few board members who had seen it had raised some opposition.

"He asked me to return the next week. When I did, I was thinking, 'Surely the Lord will bless us and allow me to have the film this week.' But the secretary simply said to me, 'I cannot give you the film yet because you must obtain special permission from the minister.'

"The minister he referred to is the Minister of Information and Broadcasting and serves as the chairman of the censor board. He is also a devout Muslim. As I started to leave, a member of the censor board invited me to his home. There he expressed his desire for this film to be shown throughout the country. He said, 'This is an excellent film and you must show it everywhere – to Christians and non-Christians alike!' He further explained that the censor board members were trying to prevent the censor certificate from being issued because they feared it would be shown outside the church buildings. They were sure, upon viewing this film, that many people would receive Jesus Christ. However, they could find no laws by which they could stop the permission from being granted. So, this man encouraged me to talk directly with the minister.

"I went to his chamber and as we met, he encouraged me very much. He stated, 'Since this is your film, you have the right to import it. I will give you permission to import the film and use it for religious education. You can use the film within Christian premises, or within the churches."

The director concludes his story by giving glory to God for answering their prayers so abundantly. He also added that a further clarification of the ruling permits them to show the film on the grounds beside church buildings. Since many churches meet in homes, they are able to show the film in many areas of the country, with an average of 3,000 people attending each showing.

Truly, Jesus does speak Bengali, Hindi, Fijian and all the languages of the world. Because they have never seen a film before, many people in Asian villages think they are actually seeing Jesus on the screen. As Jesus speaks to them in His own words from Scripture, in their own language, they respond in unprecendented numbers. This 2,000-year-old message meets the needs of individuals today. What a tremendous responsibility it is to shepherd these millions of new believers who are entering God's kingdom as a result of seeing this film.

CHAPTER FIVE

Enlarge My Borders

Now Jabez called on the God of Israel, saying, "Oh that Thou wouldst bless me indeed, and enlarge my border, and that Thy hand might be with me, and that Thou wouldst keep me from harm, that is may not pain me!" And God granted him what he requested.

I Chronicles 4:10

Operation Jabez

God used this prayer of Jabez from the Old Testament as Campus Crusade for Christ, Philippines planned toward national gospel saturation. Claiming the request of Jabez for God to enlarge his borders, they launched their saturation program, naming it Operation Jabez (OJ). Soon OJ became a byword in Christian circles all across the country. Everyone was talking about OJ.

As a result of Operation Jabez, more than five million Filipinos were directly confronted with the claims of Christ during 1980. This means that one out of every nine of the Philippines' 47 million people were personally given the opportunity to receive Christ during those 12 months.

To implement Operation Jabez, teams were located in five areas of the Philippine Islands: northern Luzon, central Luzon, southern Luzon, the Visayas and Mindanao. Team members stayed with local church members or community leaders who had been previously contacted. From that central point in each municipality, they reached out to surrounding *barrios* (villages or communities).

The outreaches were conducted in several ways, but normally they included evangelistic film showings, meetings in schools and with community leaders, one-on-one evangelism and house-to-house flier distribution.

One of the most effective aspects of OJ has been to train local church members in how to share their faith and how to disciple others. In this way, the teams do not merely add new believers to a community, but they multiply their own lives by leaving trained Christians to continue the ministry in each area.

Apart from the Campus Crusade for Christ staff members, most of the manpower for OJ was provided by volunteers. College and high school students either went out during their vacation breaks or they "stopped out" of school for a semester or a year. Many laymen made arrangements to be away from their employment for an extended period of time so they could participate. Pastors traveled with the teams for weeks at a time. They reported being greatly blessed and encouraged as they witnessed the commitment of the OJ staff and volunteers. One pastor wrote, "One entire day would not be enough to share with you what God has done in my life through Operation Jabez. My spiritual life has been revived. I was especially thrilled to see the team having their quiet time and prayer time in spite of tiredness. I am challenged to do the same."

The Philippines varies greatly in density of population, primarily due to the accessibility of different areas. The largest film showing in the country had more than 30,000 in attendance and the smallest probably had 10 or 12 people.

Isolation has both advantages and disadvantages. This was discovered by one OJ team working along the coastal area of Isabela province, when they set out to take the good news of Jesus Christ to the four municipalities cut off from the rest of Luzon by mountains and sea.

The disadvantage was that they either had to hike for five days over the mountains, or go by sea in a boat that was not very sturdy. They chose the boat.

The advantages were in the form of publicity and the opportunity to see God's provision. Since there are few visitors in this area, everyone knew it when the team arrived in each *barrio*. Very little had to be done to tell people about the film, "Jesus."

Thus, team members had more time to communicate the gospel one-on-one, to village leaders and educators in small groups.

One of the most unique groups of people with whom the team came in contact was that of the Dumagat families. The Dumagats are a Negrito people, short and dark-skinned. Their ancestors are believed to have been the first inhabitants of the Philippine Islands. Through tribal wars and slave trading, their numbers have dwindled to only about 1,000 in all of the Philippines. The Dumagats now living in this region of Isabela number around 300.

The Negritos' native religion involves belief in one god, a creator, but they do not have a name for him. Their beliefs also include good and evil spirits. The OJ team had the opportunity of showing "Jesus" to a group of 30 people in Tagalog, a language the Dumagats understand. Although they had heard a little about Christ and the Bible in the past, these people had many questions about the film and were very open in talking about spiritual things.

The team encountered the same spiritual openness throughout this isolated area, with some 2,500 other people viewing "Jesus" in Tagalog and Ilocano. In many locations, people requested that a pastor come to establish an evangelical church, because none existed in their area. They offered to provide land, and to help with lumber and labor for the pastor to build his home.

OJ Goes International

OJ also had an international flavor when 201 American staff, students and graduates joined the project. Sixty-four of these students were participants in the first "Stop-Out" for Christ project, a year-long opportunity to serve the Lord overseas in a full-time ministry of evangelism and discipleship.

After nine months of ministering in Guam and in the islands of Micronesia, and with a desire to enlarge their borders even further, the "Stop-Out" for Christ team journeyed to the Philippines. Joined by 137 additional summer project volunteer staff and students, they participated in the saturation of the Philippines with the gospel.

Joining the central Luzon OJ project already in operation, they formed 25 teams to fan out across the central plains of that island, the largest of the nation. In eight-day cycles, they took

"Jesus" to towns and *barrios* all across their area. In one eight-day cycle alone, nearly 150,000 people heard the claims of Christ through film showings, classroom presentations and personal evangelism.

The members of the international staff were especially impressed with the people's hunger to know God. One night shortly before a film showing was to begin in a village, a hard rainstorm hit. The film team considered canceling the showing, but had to reconsider when they saw a crowd of 200 people gathering in the rain. They quickly improvised protection for the equipment by placing it in the back of a covered jeep. For two-and-a-half hours, 200 people stood in the rain, watching the life of Christ on film, and learning how they could know Him in a personal way.

This group of Filipino and American staff and students was used to expose almost 700,000 people to the claims of Christ during their two-month stint with OJ.

God constantly proved Himself trustworthy to supply the team members' needs, which were many and varied. Promised operational funds and allowances for volunteers often did not come. There were times when it seemed a team was sure to be stranded in an area due to a lack of funds. But, as one OJ staff exclaimed, "God never failed us. Sacrifices were made. There were cuts in allowances. But no one missed a meal and no one was forced to walk for financial reasons. One of the many precious lessons we learned was that we could trust God. We found Him able, and absolutely worthy of our fullest trust."

God demonstrated His faithfulness for four consecutive nights during the film showing in one area. Each day the rain continued to threaten the scheduled showings, but by the time the film began, the darkened skies gave way to bright twinkling stars and the waiting people in this area were able to hear about His personal love for them.

The staff of Philippine Campus Crusade for Christ accepted the task of saturating the country with the claims of Christ with great seriousness. The national director, a former army colonel, informed the staff members that they would be involved in spiritual combat throughout their saturation project. He listed three personal requirements for them to follow: (1) those who were single were to remain single, (2) those who were married were to practice family planning and (3) good physical condition of all staff members was to be maintained at any cost.

During the saturation, several staff members became very ill, mainly due to poor quality of food and water to which they were continually exposed. However, God honored their faith and obedience and through this project five million Filipinos were confronted with Jesus Christ.

Throughout Operation Jabez, as I read stories that came to my desk, I was often overwhelmed with the impact these OJ staff people and volunteers were having in their country. In my opinion, very few things are as exciting as individual lives being transformed when they come in contact with the living Savior, Jesus Christ. Stories that thrill me continue to come in every day.

For instance, an 18-year-old OJ volunteer from Padada, Davao del Sur, contacted 85 people and all indicated that they had prayed to receive Christ. This occurred during the three days in which the volunteer was being trained in how to witness.

In another instance, two days after a high school student from North Cotabato received Christ through an OJ team leader, she took an excessive amount of sleeping pills in an attempt to take her own life. Coming from a broken home, she felt she could no longer stand the tension in her home. However, by God's grace, her life was spared.

The OJ team leader who led her to Christ went to visit her. This was the beginning of several sessions with her and her family. In the process, the student's father trusted Christ as his Lord and Savior. Then her mother recommitted her life to Jesus Christ. Both parents admitted that the way in which they related to one another and the way in which they conducted their family life was wrong. For the first time since their marriage, they asked forgiveness of each other. Then, to the amazement of the team leader, the girl's father took the mother's hand and they each expressed their love to the other. The entire family life has since been radically transformed.

A church in North Cotabato has baptized more than 75 people since its involvement with OJ and another church in Sultan Kudarat, where the pilot OJ project in Southern Mindanao was conducted, has doubled its membership.

Literally hundreds of mayors and city officials across the Philippines have received Christ this year since these leaders were the first to be contacted when the teams advanced into a new area.

After seeing the film in the town plaza of a north Cotabato

city, one of the city officials was very antagonistic and actually cursed the film. A few days later this judge became very ill. As he was suffering, he remembered that Christ had suffered for him on the cross. He called for a local pastor to visit him, and as a result he prayed to receive Christ. The pastor is now conducting a Bible study in the home of this judge.

God faithfully kept the OJ team members from harm. Many of the towns in which the teams had ministered either experienced political fighting between the military and rebels, or were bombed after the teams left.

On one occasion, though, a bomb exploded during a film showing where several thousand people were present. Fortunately, no one was injured, but the majority of the audience ran away. The staff prayed about what they should do, and they felt led to turn the projector back on. Immediately, a larger crowd than before gathered to watch the remainder of the film.

Captive Audiences

God has enlarged our borders in unusual ways in other countries as well. One of these exciting ways is through our film ministry to Cambodians, Vietnamese and Laotians located in refugee camps in Thailand.

When we originally began the translation work for "Jesus," I immediately asked Taing Vek Huong, our staff member who had miraculously escaped the genocide of Cambodia after four years of captivity, to translate this film into Cambodian. Since the Thai and Laotian languages are very similar in spoken form, we would be able to use our Thai prints among Laotian refugees.

During my previously-described visit to Khao I Dong refugee camp, it was apparent that I needed to assign a staff member to minister among these refugees for the next few months. I selected an American who had been involved in our ministry for a number of years. During the last six months of 1980, under his leadership, 142,000 refugees were personally confronted with the claims of Christ through the use of "Jesus."

The first item our staff member needed was the Four Spiritual Laws booklet translated in Cambodian language. We printed 100,000 copies. Then he began the lengthy process of getting permission to enter the camps.

In spite of a limited supply of materials and an inability to speak the language, he set out to multiply his life spiritually inside the camps. He asked a Cambodian pastor to arrange for the use of the church in the camp for training a group of refugees in personal evangelism. He expected a few dozen people to attend this initial training session, but upon his arrival, he found 400 Christians waiting to be trained! In addition to the basic training course given to these 400, he was able to disciple 18 of them to become leaders who, in turn, could train others.

Later, our staff member related an incident from the pastor's life. Before his escape to Thailand, this Cambodian pastor's home was situated so that the Khmer Rouge passed it on their way home from late night meetings. One day, one of them asked him, "Who are those people dressed in white who stand beside your house each night?" The pastor then knew that God was miraculously protecting him. He also shared that there always seemed to be food of some kind wherever he was, and that he was not made to suffer like so many others had been. Our staff member stated, "I was greatly impressed with this living demonstration of the Twenty-third Psalm and the way God continually protected and provided for this man's needs."

God also protected the Christians while "Jesus" was being shown in the camps. On one occasion, it was shown at a children's day care center which was operated by a Christian couple. About half of the children began to weep loudly when the crucifixion scene was shown. The couple were worried that something might happen to them if the children were heard crying. They were aware of the fact that certain officials felt that since Cambodia was traditionally a Buddhist nation, any effort to communicate the gospel should be prohibited. Later, the couple discovered no one had heard the crying children, so they were able to continue their ministry with them.

The frequent attempts to repatriate those who volunteered to go back to Cambodia were harrowing. Cambodians were taken away from the camps in buses and brought back in ambulances, because they were often caught in the crossfire of the Thai and Vietnamese. I was told that once they were back inside Cambodia, the Vietnamese would surround them, saying, "We know you are Khmer Rouge," and would begin to stab them with knives. One day while watching them board the buses, one of our Thai-speaking staff members overheard a Thai guard say, "These people are going back to die." For many of them this was true.

This fact alone impresses me with the urgency of the hour in getting the good news of Jesus Christ to those inside these camps. And, again, I am grateful that God has supplied a workable strategy to help reach the thousands of refugees who are in desperate need of a Savior. Praise the Lord with me that at least 142,000 refugees have been exposed to His wonderful plan of redemption through seeing the film, "Jesus," in their own language.

REFUGEE MINISTRY STATISTICS
(six months of 1980)

REFUGEE CAMP	NUMBER ATTENDING "JESUS" FILM	NATIONALITY
Khao I Dong	68,650	Khmer (Cambodian)
Old Aranyaprathet	2,500	Khmer
Sakeo	17,500	Khmer
Mairut	8,000	Khmer
Nong Khai	3,450	Lao
Ban Vinai	15,400	Lao
Sikew	1,500	Vietnamese
Kamput	5,000	Khmer
Suan Plu	500	Khmer
Lumpini	2,200	Khmer/Lao
Loei	15,000	Lao
Bataan (Philippines)	3,000	Vietnamese
TOTAL	142,900	

They Came by Canoe

There are few places where people have been more responsive to the gospel message presented through the film, "Jesus," than the island nations of the Pacific. Where the film has been shown, 60% to 75% of entire nations have viewed it.

This film is enabling us to accomplish one of our major objectives in the South Pacific, by helping to saturate the entire population of these scattered islands with the gospel. Already islanders have come to see the film in great numbers, and thousands have prayed by faith to receive Christ into their lives.

Following a preview of the film held for church leaders in Fiji, the secretary of the Bible Society for Melanesia and Polynesia recognized the great potential of the film for use across Fiji. He suggested we produce a special edition of the Gospel of Luke to distribute at the film presentations. This special edition has proved to be one of the most effective evangelistic tools presently being produced in the South Pacific. Inexpensively reproduced on newsprint, it contains Luke's Gospel with photos from the film. It also includes the Four Spiritual Laws, and material for three follow-up Bible studies and the booklet entitled "Have You Made the Wonderful Discovery of the Spirit-filled Life?" In conjunction with the Bible Society, we have printed 500,000 copies of this booklet in nine languages.

The booklet is being used well in individual follow-up. When a person receives it, he has a portion of the Scripture, and an explanation of how to make a personal commitment to Christ, how to be sure of that commitment, initial steps in how to grow, how to be filled with the Holy Spirit by faith and how to continue walking in fellowship with Christ.

Many families are using the booklet in their family devotions. Even if we are only able to show the film and place one of these booklets in every home, we believe a tremendous spiritual awakening will take place on these islands as a result.

Twenty film teams operated for four months in the Solomon Islands. These islands have a very isolated, widely-distributed population of 221,000 people. During those four months, reports indicated that 166,000 people, or 75% of the total population, saw the film. Approximately 40% of those indicated they had prayed by faith to invite Christ into their lives.

A unique strategy is used in these islands. The film teams bring the people together in what they call "heap-up" villages. These are smaller villages which have simply grouped together to form a larger village. An advance team arrives by canoe or by a path over the mountains several days ahead to promote the film and gather the heap-up village. Then the film team arrives, ready to show a full-color movie to people who have never seen an electric light, or even a black and white photo. It is such a novelty to see a projector, film or screen that the film must be shown more than once in every location. The first time, the audience is fascinated with seeing the film itself. The second time they listen to the message.

The team then spends two additional days in the heap-up village. With little else to do, the people willingly go through the follow-up booklet in all-day teaching sessions. Before leaving, the team shows the film again in order to help solidify each person's understanding of his commitment to Christ.

One village in the Solomon Islands had been resettled after an earthquake. This caused the people to feel insecure, resulting in unrest, drunkeness, immorality and crime throughout the village. Even though church leaders had little hope for this village and referred to it as a dead village, "Jesus" was shown there. Following the showing, ninety-eight percent of these distressed villagers indicated they had committed their lives to Christ. They began to gather each evening to sing, share, study the Bible and have fellowship. The life of the village is totally transformed because they have found security in Christ. Now, several months later, they are still rejoicing in how their lives were changed the night "Jesus" came to the village.

The archbishop of the Church of Melanesia, which is the largest denomination in the Solomon Islands, recently shared that all the plans and strategies they are implementing emphasize a personal commitment to Christ and consistent Christian living. He continued by saying, "Our new emphasis is a direct result of the ministry of Campus Crusade and especially their strategy in using the film 'Jesus.'" Many of his church leaders freely indicated that they personally received Christ at a film showing.

This archbishop spent two months personally transporting the film teams in his own ship. Government ships do not travel to one isolated group of islands with a population of 11,000, so the archbishop arranged to transport the team himself. He stated a total of 8,000 of these Islanders saw the film. Streams of canoes followed his ship from island to island in order to see the film over and over again. The last showing was held on the airstrip of the major island where 4,000 people attended. Following the conclusion of the film, the islanders remained seated for another hour without moving. Many wept as they reflected on the impact the film had had on their lives. Certainly the borders of this Solomon Island church have been greatly enlarged.

The Governor General of Fiji, who is the British Crown's representative, agreed to come to a special showing of "Jesus." Since the Governor General was the guest of honor, all the government ministers, the legislative council and all department heads also attended this showing.

When the Prime Minister, who was out of the country, returned and discovered he had missed the film, he requested another special showing be held in his home for him and his family.

In this central area of the main island of Fiji, after viewing the film, an elderly man remarked, "I am so thankful that God has kept me alive for 103 years! Today, I heard the gospel and accepted Christ. If I die tomorrow, I don't need to worry about it anymore."

Fiji is known for its torrential rains. However, during the 443 film showings held there, not one was rained out. As the first words flashed across the screen, the rain stopped and the weather was dry throughout the presentation.

In Papua New Guinea the three major trade languages, Pidgin, Hiri Motu and English, are understood by 60% of the population, even though more than 700 languages are spoken there. Recently, when the Here's Life, Port Moresby campaign was conducted, "Jesus" was effectively used to communicate the gospel with 33,800 people. Of those, 6,760 indicated that they received Christ into their lives. Approximately 900 have joined Bible study groups.

In other areas of Papua New Guinea, during a three-month period more than 10,000 people saw the film. Twelve hundred of those people indicated decisions for Christ.

On October 31, 1980 the Royal Premiere of "Jesus" was held in Tonga for His Majesty King Taufa'ahaw Tupou IV. This launched the film strategy in this island kingdom. The film, in the Tongan language, reached more than 50% of the population of 110,000 people in only two months' time.

Another exciting aspect of the film strategy is the way in which it is used to unite Christian groups in the common goal of saturating a country with the gospel. In the Pacific Islands, yachts have been offered by many groups to help transport film teams from island to island. Other types of vehicles have also been volunteered for land travel. Most encouraging are the volunteer workers who give of their time and resources to help saturate their nation. The responsiveness of even non-Christian groups have been overwhelming.

In Sri Lanka our staff observed that 90% of the help offered in the rural film strategy came from Buddhists. This included the use of a small bedroom to shelter our projector during a rainstorm. The two-hour film was shown through the bedroom window onto a cloth screen tied between two coconut trees in the compound. During that showing 150 people standing beneath umbrellas were exposed to the gospel. Often Buddhists generously offered electricity and meals to the film team members, and they willingly assisted the film teams in preparing for the show.

The knowledge that lives are being changed through hearing and accepting the beautiful message of God's love and forgiveness makes such strategies fulfilling and gives us the incentive to continue enlarging our borders. For example, in Dangedora, Sri Lanka, a rough appearing man sauntered up to a film team member demanding to know what he was doing. Then he asked if he could help him in any way. A little unsure of this man's motive, the team member asked if he knew where he could find electricity for the projector. To the team member's delight, the man replied that he was an electrician and he eagerly began to help set up the equipment for the film showing. At the conclusion of the film he was the first one to turn in his comment card. You guessed it! He prayed to receive Christ as he heard the gospel message through the film showing.

In Matara, Sri Lanka, five young men from a nearby village prayed to receive Christ with our staff members after a showing of "Jesus." Faithfully, all five attended the three follow-up appointments. A short time later, they led our film team to their own village and made arrangements for the film to be shown to the entire village.

An unspeakable privilege has been ours, as our borders have been enlarged during 1980. Wherever our ministry has taken us, we have found people to be exceedingly hungry to know God. And, when presented with the gospel in a clear, loving manner, thousands respond positively.

After Jabez had prayed for his borders to be enlarged, the Scripture tells us, "And God granted him what he requested."

Young boy listens intently to the gospel as campaign worker shares the good news during Here's Life, Macau.

During Here's Life, Taegu, Korean campaign workers used sandwich boards to bring new life in Christ to attention of the people in their area.

Below: Korean girl learns about new life in Christ during Here's Life, Korea.

Jing Avillaneda, staff trainee from the Philippines, spoke to members of the seven-family community of Paloming when the team visited nearby San Carlos. Jing spoke in Tagalog so all could understand.

Below: Operation Jabez team of American Stop Out students and Philippine staff members hike with student volunteers to the area where film will be shown.

Korean Christians catch catnaps after an all-night prayer rally during the 1980 World Evangelization Crusade.

Below: Operation Jabez outreach team that went into four remote municipalities of the Filipino province of Isabela frequently traveled by *bangka* as they went from place to place showing the "Jesus" film.

Eye-catching display in the cinema lobby attracts passersby.

Dr. Bill Bright, with the pastor as interpreter, speaks to congregation of Young Nak Presbyterian Church on Sunday before 1980 World Evangelization Crusade begins.

Large groups of school children wait for buses to take them back to school after showing of "Jesus" film.

In addition to the huge mass rallies held each evening on Yoido Plaza, churches in Seoul were filled daily during the week of the '80 World Evangelization Crusade as people came to the day-time conference sessions.

Village staff members simulate hike to an outreach point.

Below: During Operation Jabez, the path to a village was often blocked by a river, which meant wading or swimming. Here Filipino student volunteers, staff members and Stop Out students cross river on their way to a "Jesus" showing.

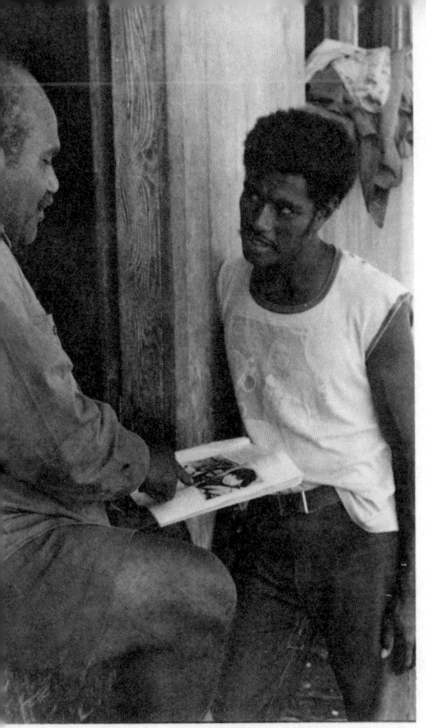

Fiji's "Jesus" film strategy included the Gospel of Luke printed on newsprint, with the Four Spiritual Laws and some Bible studies. A team member discusses the book with another man.

Opportunities to share the gospel are frequent. Here a Stop Out student shares the Four Spiritual Laws with a tricycle driver in the Philippines.

Singaporean volunteer *(right)* is one of those who went into four remote municipalities in Isabela to help share the gospel there. Here she talks with a woman and child who are members of the Dumagat tribe, a group of negrito people.

Children wait patiently for film showing in this rural Philippine area.

Below: Part of the preparation for a "Jesus" film showing is the strategic placement of posters advertising the movie. Filipino, Stop Out student, volunteers assist with the work.

CHAPTER SIX

I Hiked 30 Kilometers Today

"I hiked 30 kilometers today," said an American nurse serving on our staff in the Philippines. It is not such a great feat to hike 30 kilometers (18 miles) in one day, unless it happens to be on narrow paths leading through rice paddies, and then up a slippery mountain trail, as part of a team hand-carrying a gasoline generator, a 16mm movie projector, speakers, films and boxes and boxes of materials. And, unless, on top of this, you have done the same thing every day for the last week!

Fortunately, our film teams and operation Jabez staff members did not have to walk that distance every day, but for much of 1980, this was a common occurrence for the teams that were spread across the continent.

Much has already been shared about the results of the showings of the film, "Jesus," during late 1980 in Asia and the Pacific Islands. We have seen God use these obedient, trusting staff members and volunteers in a mighty way. However, at this time, let's join an actual film team about to depart from their home base in Illagan, Isabella, in the Philippines to participate in an eight-day Operation Jabez cycle in the municipality of Santiago. This is their 14th of 31 OJ cycles this year.

Put on your jeans, some comfortable walking shoes and let's go. Don't forget your insect repellent and a good supply of Lomotil!

It is the morning of Day One in the municipality of Santiago. Since this is one of the larger commercial areas of the province, this film team has been assigned two projectors, one generator, one car battery, one slide projector, one Ilocano language film, one film in English, one "Jesus" filmstrip, a sound system and eight boxes of materials. Most of the early morning hours are spent loading the equipment and luggage onto a rented jeepney, and it will take two hours to ride from their home base to the city of Santiago. The team of 12 includes two Campus Crusade village staff men and four village staff women, two male and two female student volunteers and two American nurses. Four of the team members went ahead last night because the passengers and equipment wouldn't all fit into one jeepney.

In Santiago, they will be guests of the largest denominational church in the area. The eight girls will sleep in the pastor's house and the four men will sleep on hard, wooden pews inside the church.

Arriving at 11 a.m., they are greeted by the pastor and his wife. As the team leader talks to the pastor about the week's schedule – already set up by an advance team – the women begin to prepare lunch over an open fire behind the parsonage. Local Christians have donated firewood and rice for their use. The team buys fish and vegetables from the local market to complete their meal.

After lunch a staff meeting is conducted by the team leader, who goes over the schedule and makes assignments for the evangelism and discipleship training to be held on Sunday. Two film showings have already been set up for tonight. One place has electricity and is located along the national highway so the team should not experience an electricity or transportation problem. However, the other location is an hour away, has no electricity and transportation only goes into the area twice eacy day. A small team is quickly assigned to go. They hurry to organize their equipment and gather their luggage before they miss the last ride. They will spend the night there and return to Santiago on the first ride in the morning. Only three team members are sent to this location since it covers only three small *barrios*. The remainder of the team is needed for the larger area.

Santiago is large, and the team decides where to hold additional film showings in the surrounding *barrios* based on their location and population. The team leader assigns three women to contact and make arrangements with local college and high school officials to show the film to the students during the day.

They are also to request approval to hold evangelistic meetings for the teachers.

The other six team members are sent to promote tonight's film showing in two large *barrios* which will be combined. Since the *barrios* are situated along the highway, two team members attach a loud speaker to a tricycle (motorcycle with a side car used for public transportation) and drive through the two *barrios,* announcing the details of the film showing. The remaining four members go from house to house throughout the *barrios,* handing out fliers containing the Four Spiritual Laws and advertisements of the film, "Jesus."

The nine team members rejoin in their "home" in the late afternoon. They have just enough time to cool off, clean up and change clothes before leaving for the film showing. Two women are left behind to prepare supper, which will be eaten much later tonight. The film is scheduled to start at 7:00 p.m. but the team doesn't arrive until 6:45 so they are just a little late getting started.

As one of the American nurses begins to operate the projector, she estimates the crowd to be about 1,000. Since they do not speak the language, americans are often assigned to operate the projector and handle the behind-the-scenes details. There is a big problem with insects swarming into the projector tonight. By the end of the third reel this begins to affect the sound a little but the team prays that they will be able to finish the film. The Lord honors their prayer. During the evangelistic closing of the film, many in the audience are heard praying aloud when viewers are given an opportunity to accept Christ.

Most of the crowd leaves within a few minutes after the show ends because they must walk back to their homes. A few remain to talk and ask questions. Again, the Americans begin loading equipment so the Filipinos can be free to talk personally with the people who stay. As she is putting the equipment away, one of the nurses has found someone who can speak English. This young man explains that he has already attended one of the OJ film showings in a nearby municipality. He had prayed to receive Christ, so our staff member takes the opportunity to share with him about his need to grow spiritually and have fellowship. She invites him to attend church on Sunday so he can meet other Christians living in Santiago and to attend the upcoming training classes so he can learn to share his faith with others.

At 11 p.m. the team returns home, and by 1 a.m. they finish eating, praying together and are ready for bed. They agree that the day has been so hot they won't be able to sleep unless they cool off by washing away some of the stickiness! This is accomplished at the hand water pump located behind the pastor's house. For most of this province, indoor plumbing is only a dream.

Over the past six months of Operation Jabez the team has learned the absolute necessity of spending time alone with God, and then spending time together studying the Word and praying. Several team members begin Day Two with a 5 a.m. quiet time with God, because it is their turn to prepare breakfast and clean up. The others begin their day between 5:30 and 6:00. All meet for breakfast in time to finish before the group devotions and prayer time at 8 a.m. With everything that can go wrong during a day, they have found that their activities and health must be brought before the Lord each morning. Then, if a film showing fails to take place or something happens that they do not anticipate, they know that God is taking the responsibility for it. Following devotions, announcements are made and team members receive their assignments for the day.

One of the women who contacted school officials shares with the others that they were able to schedule film showings in one high school and two colleges, one of which also includes a high school. In one college, they also have an appointment to meet with the faculty members. At 2 p.m. this afternoon a film showing is scheduled at a large high school of about 2,000 students. The school official in charge is requiring all students to attend.

The team leader assigns one of the male team members to accompany the three women to help carry the equipment. Since the electricity is turned off all day, they need to take along a generator. The team jokingly informs us, "Even when the electricity is on, it is none too steady!"

Remember the three team members who spent the night in the distant *barrio?* They return near the end of devotions—just in time for new assignments. The staff meeting is extended for a few minutes so they can share how God had worked in their three-*barrio*-wide film showing. They relate that upon arriving there, the three met the captain (community leader) of the central *barrio* where the film was to be shown and then went to a different *barrio* to distribute Four Spiritual Laws fliers and announce the film showing. They had to hike nearly five kilometers to the nearby *barrios.*

The team seemed a little disappointed that only 150 people attended, but rejoiced that half of those who did attend indicated they had received Christ. The team used the time afterward to help the new Christians understand assurance of salvation, so it was almost 3 a.m. before they were able to sleep.

The same three-member team is again assigned today to a mountainous area that is inaccessible by transportation. They plan to take the slide projector to use for promotion, but the pastor explained that the houses are scattered, so it will be difficult to gather many people at one time. So, the team leaves with only evangelistic materials to hand out. They plan to hike the 15 kilometers back out today, since the area has such a small population and they can cover it quickly.

The rest of the team learns that there will be no electricity this evening. Two simultaneous showings are scheduled, and they were counting on the use of electricity for one of them. Yesterday the team leader talked with the two barrio captains and they personally made the arrangements so he really doesn't want to cancel either of the showings. The leader decides to hold the two film showings anyway, but the schedules one after the other. To cut down on the two and one-half hours it normally takes to show the film, they will show only the first, third and fourth reels.

The team again parts for the day and goes to promote the film and to share the gospel person-to-person. As they leave, the team leader explains, "Each time we go out to promote the film, our goal is to leave a Four Spiritual Laws flier in every home. If we have a big area to cover, we ask children to help us go to every home. We give them 'Jesus' posters, which show the time and location of the film showing on the front, and the Four Spiritual Laws on the back. Off they go, doing a much more thorough job than we could ever do alone. This also gives us more time to share Christ individually with the people."

In the meantime, the three girls visit the mayor to confirm the large *poblacion* (county seat) film showing on Saturday, only two days away. They discover that he has forgotten to reserve the large sports arena, and he doesn't think he can get it now, but he will try. The team returns to the church and spends some time in prayer, claiming meaningful portions of Scripture. The prayer goal was for a crowd of 5,000 to attend the *poblacion* showing and the arena is the only place large enough to hold that many people.

Before going to the high school to set up the equipment for the showing there, they return to the mayor's office to find out if he has been able to acquire the sports area. To the mayor's amazement, the people in charge of the arena have agreed that the film can be shown there on Saturday night. That gives these women an opening to tell him how God continually goes before them on each OJ cycle to work out problems. The mayor is a member of the church where the team is staying, but, he says, "I have never seen people actually use the kind of faith I read of in the Bible." The women are excited to see God not only answer their prayer, but use the circumstances to show this key leader of the community that faith in God can have results as real today as they were two thousand years ago.

They reach the high school an hour ahead of time, but by the time the equipment is set up, students seem to be everywhere. The principal of the school tells the team that all 2,000 students, plus the faculty, are attending the film showing. Just before the film starts, the team gathers around the projector to pray for the showing – especially that the sound system will be adequate since there were having some difficulty getting it to function today. Everything goes smoothly until toward the end of the second reel. Suddenly, the sound system goes out.

In walks a janitor who informs the team that the school has a public address system they can use, but it will take him a few minutes to set it up. They decide to share personal testimonies now rather than following the second reel change in order to hold the attention of the students. Later the American nurse will reminisce "As I went to the stage to give my three-minute personal testimony – stretched into whatever time was needed to get the PA system set up – I prayed for the ability to shout slowly and clearly so the students could understand me." Although the students in this school are taught English, they have difficulty understanding it unless it is spoken slowly and in a very simplified way. Fortunately, the students are so intrigued by listening to the blonde American that they are quiet and attentive.

"At the end of about eight minutes of shouting, the PA system was ready," she continued, "I could hardly talk by the time I sat down, but I was grateful that the attention of the students was kept. And, I know the faculty sitting in the front heard and understood my testimony of how God has changed my life through a personal relationship with Jesus Christ."

As the film showing ends, the principal relates her excitement about the film and asks if other materials are available. She wants them for the teachers of the religion classes to use to help the students better understand what they saw. She looks over the follow-up materials and the team arranges to send her enough copies for every instructor. The team is greatly encouraged that the entire high school will be studying the follow-up series in their religion classes. They will even have examinations covering this material!

Now it is already time to set up for the two major film showings and to encounter more situations in which to trust God. Trying to fit everything and everyone into a small jeep is the first hurdle. After taking out the front passenger seat to put the generator in, two people sit in the driver's seat. Then two more people squeeze into the back with the projector, boxes of materials, and sound equipment. The fifth team member sits on the generator. With this feat accomplished they leave for the two film showings. They know that the first showing is to be held for several small *barrios* at the foot of the mountains. They drive and drive and drive. The roads get worse and worse and worse. Finally, they arrive – only a half hour late! Two thousand people are waiting. With the help of these *barrio* people, they soon start the film.

The hospitality of the *barrio* folks often impresses and encourages the team. Tonight they are served refreshments during the film.

The team members are thankful that they remembered to bring their insect repellent because they are already badly bitten from the night before. The projector is turned on, and here comes the mosquitos and little moths. As they swarm in and around the projector, the girl operating it tries to fan them away. But by the end of the first reel the sound is beginning to slow down. She prays desperately for a solution as she changes the reel, quickly cleaning out as many bugs as possible. Skipping the second reel and starting the third, she suddenly remembers the insect repellent she used on herself. She liberally applies the repellent to the projector. The solution works, and the sound lasts throughout the film.

However, during the last scene of the film, the generator stops and the team can't get it started again. They don't know what to do because another large *barrio* full of people is already waiting to see the film.

By faith, they load everything back into the jeep and leave for the next *barrio.* Puzzled as to how they can show the film with the generator broken and no replacement parts available, they pray all the way. As they arrive and unload the equipment, they see a crowd of about 3,000 people waiting.

The team leader prays, "Lord, I know You will not allow anything to keep these people from hearing about Your Son." He turns the equipment on. Both the projector and generator run perfectly and 3,000 people are introduced to the person of Jesus Christ!

Receiving their assignments for Day Three, the team rejoices in how God's hand constantly moves before them and prepares the way. He proved that last night when He caused the generator to run again.

This morning a group will put up "Jesus" posters advertising the film showing to be held in the *poblacion* the next day. Another group will be preparing for the film showing at one of the colleges. High school students and several *barrios* are also being invited to attend.

The showing at the college has some unexpected blessings. First it is indoors and the gymnasium is large. Second, the school has its own generator and sound system. To see such a large gymnasium in the province is very rare.

Another team leaves just after lunch to go to an outlying *barrio.* They will stay overnight since transportation is difficult to find after 7 p.m.

Today they are supposed to have met with the faculty at a college. However, when they arrive they find that the president has forgotten to inform the faculty. So, he reschedules the time for Monday afternoon and makes an announcement. Learning to be flexible, to reschedule and rethink, has become an everyday occurrence for this OJ team.

It starts to rain around noon, but the team members roll up their pant legs, put on rubber slippers, and head out to promote the film to be shown at the other college in town. Four members go in two teams to the two nearby *barrios* to invite the people to attend the showing in the host *barrio.*

Another team of three members goes to the college to check on arrangements for using the generator and PA system. A few hundred fliers have already been left to be passed out to the students. To the team's joy, the president has done that, and further informs them that most of the people in the *barrio* already know of the film through the students.

Because of the students' unsolicited help, the team is able to cover the area quickly. This saves them a long walk in the rain, and they are able to rest for a short while before the film showing.

Eight hundred people come to the film showing at the college. Five hundred are students. A few of the students saw the film the day before and have come to see it again. One OJ volunteer stated, "It is not uncommon to find some young people who attend as many film showings in the area as possible. And they usually bring their friends with them."

It continues to rain throughout the evening. As a result, only fifty people gather to see the film in the small *barrio* where the team stayed overnight.

Other than the problem with rain, both teams report a smooth time. "So what's new, if we are soaked to the bone," quips one drenched village staff member.

It rains all night. It is still raining in the morning as the team meets for devotions on Day Four. Time is spent praying for the film showing and for team members' health. Half the team has developed dysentery because of parasites in the food and water. This is a constant battle on OJ and is a constant drain on one's energy. After devotions the two American nurses trek off to the local pharmacy to buy a new supply of Lomotil for everyone's dysentery. The other ten members divide the six *barrios* of the *poblacion* into four sections and go out to distribute fliers and announce the film showings that night. In the afternoon, since most of the team is sick, they rest for several hours. The two healthy members attach the loud-speaker to a tricycle and, along with the pastor, drive throughout the *poblacion*, announcing the film showing to be held in the big sports arena.

Even though it continues to rain heavily, a crowd of 1,000 people attends this evening's film showing. Halfway through, the electricity goes off but the generator quickly has the film rolling again. They see that even though the crowd is smaller than the anticipated 5,000, God has used the rain to bring those who are really interested in hearing how they can know Christ in a personal way. The team also expresses their thankfulness that they have only one showing tonight. This enables the ones with whom the Lomotil did not work to stay home and regain their strength.

Day Five starts even earlier than usual. It is Sunday and the team is scheduled to conduct training in evangelism and discipleship in two churches. The early morning hours are spent in prayer. The team conducting the training at the smaller *barrio* church has to leave immediately following prayer time.

In the larger church, during Sunday school, four training seminars are led by Filipino team members. One American staff member is assigned to teach the professionals since they want their training in English. She really enjoys this experience and is excited when several attorneys and college professors become enthusiastic about learning how to share their faith with others in an effective way. One attorney asks, "How can I be sure that someone has really prayed to receive Christ?" The seminar leader explains to him that his responsibility is simply to tell others about Christ. It is God's responsibility to actually draw men to Himself and cause them to understand and respond to the gospel as the attorney shares with them. When he understands that the result of his sharing is God's responsibility, not his, this attorney has a whole new outlook about sharing Christ.

The entire day is spent in training sessions with only a short break for lunch and a rest break in the afternoon. As people return to their homes in the afternoon to rest, they are challenged to bring at least one family with them to the film showing at the church that night.

That evening more than 300 people crowd into the church. About halfway through the third reel, the electricity goes off. They don't have a generator because the other team has taken it to the smaller *barrio* church. The team begins to pray that God will cause the electricity to be turned back on. Almost all of the people stay seated, singing and sharing with one another by candlelight. An hour later, the power comes on and they are able to finish the film. The team is grateful for this extra time of fellowship with the church.

When both teams arrive home late Sunday night, it is discovered that 20 individuals attended the morning worship service in the small church. Only 5 remained for the showing that evening.

On Monday, Day Six, the host pastor leads the morning devotions for the team. "Until Sunday," explains the team leader, "the pastor kept a little more removed from our activities than most pastors have. But during our devotions, he told us how our life-style had impressed him and the people of his church. It was as though they had been watching us to see if we live what we talk about."

Following devotions, one team leaves with the generator and other equipment. They are going for a film showing in a group of *barrios* located in the mountaineous part of the municipality. They are told it can be reached by some means of transportation. They have already hiked to many places accessible only by foot. They are to be gone for two nights and because of the heavy rains of the weekend, they might need to hike into more of these areas.

Right after the assignments are given, the women go to the college to check with the president and make sure the meeting with the faculty is still scheduled. The team has learned the importance of checking and rechecking to assure better results for their plans. They are able to confirm both the faculty meeting that afternoon and the film showing that evening. They also obtain permission to invite the area people to attend the showing.

In the afternoon, about 30 faculty members are present for the evangelistic team meeting. An OJ volunteer shares his personal testimony and a Campus Crusade staff member presents a short message and gives the faculty an opportunity to accept Christ. Comment cards are completed by the faculty members indicating that one-fourth of them accepted Christ into their lives by faith.

The evening at the college turns out to be a challenge for the team and they claim one of their most often-quoted promises of Scripture: "And we know that God causes all things to work together for good to those who love God, to those who are called according to His purpose" (Romans 8:28).

These times seem to come when it appears that everything is under control and things are going smoothly! This evening things do go as planned – through the end of the first reel. Then, the electricity goes off. But, the team assumes this will not be a problem as soon as they get the generator going. Again, the American nurse is called on to give her testimony. She is ready to conclude, but notices her teammates are still having trouble with the projector and are not yet ready to start the film. Since there are more than 1,000 students present, and she knows how restless students can become when they have to wait, she extends her testimony for another five minutes; then ends, hoping they are ready to start.

As she leaves the stage, she hears a whispered explanation that the generator is too strong for the projector and the projector is about to burn up. They are trying to adjust the projector so it can be used with the extra strong current.

In the meantime, the master of ceremonies gives her extended testimony and then introduces another OJ worker to give his testimony and sing a song. By the time the projector is finally ready to roll with the second reel, eight team members have told how Christ has changed their lives! They are amazed that the large crowd has quietly listened to these testimonies and very few have left.

A few minutes into the second reel the projector is again overheating, and the showing has to be stopped. A village staff member, the only one who had not previously spoken, explains why the film cannot be continued and shares the message of the film personally.

The team praises God for the situation. They see more than 1,000 people, mostly students, listen attentively to the message of the gospel instead of watching the film which they have come to see. Afterwards, one student admits, "I wish I could have seen the film, but I enjoyed hearing as both Filipinos and Americans shared their lives and how Jesus has changed them. It helped me realize that the same God works in all hearts, and a personal relationship with Christ brings the same happiness and peace to everyone."

On Day Seven the team misses the three team members who are still in the mountains on their two-day trip, so they spend extra time praying for them.

Early in the afternoon the team goes to pass out fliers in the area where the film will be shown tonight. They also announce the film showing with the loud-speaker and share Christ with the residents. The film will be shown at a site alongside the national highway with good access to transportation so they know many people will come.

Three members stay behind to cook supper and finish distributing fliers to sections of the *poblacion* where they have previously been unable to go. By this time they have reconciled to the fluctuating electricity of this particular municipality and are praying about the situation. The leader talks with the *barrio* captain who informs him that if the electricity goes off, it usually comes back on within an hour or so, and the people are usually willing to wait for it to return.

Tonight the team members are introduced to the *barangay* brigade – a village council assigned to maintain peace and order – who stay very close to the team members. During the showing, the electricity does go off, and the time is spent singing songs and sharing testimonies with the crowd of 2,000 until the electricity comes back on.

However, during this time the young people have become restless and have begun to throw stones. Later, the team learns that this is why the *barangay* brigade stayed near the OJ team. This *barrio* is known as a rough area, but the *barrio* captain had heard of the film showings and wanted his people to see this film, so he sent the brigade to protect the team.

Finally the power returns and they are able to finish the film. The *barrio* captain's appreciation reminds the team of the attitude of officials from many other rough areas. His gratitude encourages the members when he says, "I see this film as a very helpful means of reaching the people in a positive sense. It presents a wonderful solution to violence and rebellion."

Day Eight! The day to pack and go back to the home base for a three-day break. The team is waiting for their missing members to return before holding devotions.

Finally about 10 a.m. they arrive. They had a very interesting time. They were able to reach the first *barrio* by jeepney even though the roads were quite muddy. Around 200 people came to their first film showing. The next day after riding to the river which was as far as the jeepney could go in the mud, they still had to hike a kilometer before reaching the larger *barrio* where they had scheduled a showing.

After making inquiries about the best way to travel the last muddy kilometer, they decided to hire a *carabao* (water buffalo) and a cart to pull them to the location of the film showing. After loading their many pounds of equipment and materials into the small wooden cart, they climbed on top and the big animal began his slow journey up the slippery trail.

They finally reached their destination, and about 500 people attended the showing. The team also had a joyful time as they stayed in the captain's home and ministered to his family. The *barrio* captain had become a Christian and was very eager to grow in his faith.

One tired, but rejoicing, film team member said, "It is really hard to leave a place when you are leaving behind people who are baby Christians and so interested in growing. But, I realize I must keep going in order to give others the opportunity to know Christ personally."

During devotions and prayer, the team thanks God for His wonderful protection and provision and for the great things He has done in the municipality of Santiago. They joyfully report to their host pastor that approximately 14,130 people in his area have been exposed to the claims of Christ through seeing the film, "Jesus," and through attending evangelistic team meetings. Approximately 48% of them have indicated their decision to accept Christ into their lives by faith.

Following a quick lunch the weary OJ team packs up its equipment once again and begins the two-hour trip home. "Or at least our home while we are in this province," explains one member. "Actually, home is wherever we unroll our mat and hang up our mosquito net!"

* * *

Tired? I am! and I can't help but remember that this was just one of 31 similar eight-day cycles which this team and many like it undertook. Today in both large and small *barrios* of the Philippines many new believers are experiencing peace and hope for the first time in their lives. I am sure they echo the words of our Lord when He declares in Isaiah 52:7, "How lovely on the mountains are the feet of him who brings good news, who announces peace and brings good news of happiness, who announces salvation, and says to Zion, 'Your God reigns!'"

CHAPTER SEVEN

The Purified Church

That the proof of your faith, being more precious than gold which is perishable, even though tested by fire, may be found to result in praise and glory and honor at the revelation of Jesus Christ.

I Peter 1:7

The church in the People's Republic of China has been tested, tried and purified. During the past 30 years, few Christians on the face of the earth have experienced greater persecution. Today, the church in China is emerging as a vigorous body, much stronger and larger than most people imagined possible.

We can make a simple comparison by asking this question, "If someone prays for a loved one who has been critically ill and confined to bed for many years, and one day that loved one becomes well, what is the reaction?" The initial response of the one who prayed is usually one of surprise.

Even though Christians around the world have prayed faithfully for more than 30 years for the church in China, its spiritual health today has taken us by surprise. What a pleasant surprise it is! Of course, there is no way to know how many Christians there are in China, but many feel that there may be ten times as many as has been anticipated.

We are beginning to catch glimpses of what the church has endured in the past 30 years. I have heard many who are interested in China discuss the idea that this situation may have produced a type of Christian that many from the so-called free world will find difficult to understand and accept.

There appear to be two major categories of Christians in China today. One is the group of older Christians who have survived the persecution of the past 30 years and are still trusting and serving the Lord. The second group is much younger in years, and is the product of an atheistic, Marxist society. This younger generation of believers encountered the person of Jesus Christ and discovered that there is more to life than they were experiencing. They, too, are learning to trust and serve the Lord, but they are the ones who are more likely to be misunderstood.

This has been a traumatic 30 years in the life of the church in China. At the time of the Communist Revolution in 1949, Christianity as a whole was associated with western imperialism and domination. In rejection of this situation, there arose the Three-Self Patriotic Movement in 1954 and all churches were placed under its authority.

This is the same Three-Self Movement we hear so much about today. It requires all religious activity to be: (1) self-governing, (2) self-supporting, and (3) self-propagating.

In 1954 the Three-Self Movement became very political in nature, and in the years following many churches closed their doors as a result. Scattered, the believers began to meet secretly in homes. The churches cooperating with the Three-Self Movement remained open until 1966 when the Cultural Revolution exploded across China. Extreme persecution raged through both types of churches.

During this time secret house churches were the only available places of worship for believers, so they greatly increased in number. Following the death of Chairman Mao in 1976 they grew at an even faster rate. Today we are learning that the growth of home churches in China is unprecendented.

As a result of a meeting of the Chinese Christian Council in October, 1980, there is much speculation as to whether or not these thousands of house churches are considered legal by the authorities. Whether they are or not, they are growing at a phenomenal rate. At the same time, the Three-Self Movement churches are being reopened rapidly. They are filled, for the most part, with believers who desire to hear the gospel preached from these pulpits.

What a challenging and delightful turn of events this is after so many years of silence and persecution.

We have evidence that the spiritual hunger that exists in China today is as strong as it is in any other part of the world. Again, this hunger far exceeds most of our expectations. The hunger and resulting responsiveness are as prevalent for those who remain in China and hear the gospel as they are for those who travel abroad and hear about Christ in another culture.

Since my first trip to China taken in 1978 I have a personal theory regarding why the response to the gospel is much greater than we had anticipated.

Tremendous changes are taking place in China today, which are creating increased opportunities for the spread of the gospel. Even seemingly negative policies of the government have helped to prepare the hearts of the Chinese people to respond to the love of Christ.

Consider, for example, the little emphasis placed on the family unit in modern China. Children are in schools from early morning until late evening. For a family to earn a living, every adult member has to work. As a result the children are essentially raised by the State. This situation would seem to cause a real vacuum in people's lives – a lack of love, and of a close family structure.

Whether an individual is raised in a Marxist society or not, he still experiences the need to love others and the need to be loved. Those needs are largely going unmet in China today. I feel that the resulting emptiness in the lives of the people is preparing them to respond to Christ. As Chinese, who have grown up deprived of love, begin to hear about Christ and about how much God loves them, I think phenomenal things will take place, for few can resist God's dynamic, unconditional love when it has been thoroughly explained and understood.

Although I am not free to share many of the thrilling situations through which God has uniquely revealed His love to hungry hearts in China, the following stories will serve as examples of how He is working there.

Recently a young Chinese Christian spent 19 days with a tour group inside the People's Republic of China. Miss Lee (fictional name) visited six cities to "test the responses of the people in China to the gospel message as presented in the Four Spiritual Laws."

Frequently she began conversations by asking people if she could tape their local dialect. Then she gave them a copy of the

Four Spiritual Laws booklet, taped them as they read it aloud and played the recording back to them. Afterward, she answered their questions concerning the content of the booklet and gave them the opportunity to personally invite Christ into their lives.

One of her witnessing experiences occurred while she was riding a train to the Great Wall. Sitting alone in one of the cars was a man in his 60's. The day before, she had read the passage in Acts 8 concerning Philip and the Ethiopian eunuch, and this prompted her to begin a conversation with the man. As they talked, she discovered he had worked as a tour guide for 30 years.

After he had read the Four Spiritual Laws booklet, she turned to I Corinthians 13:4-7 and asked him to read this passage. After doing so, he said that this is the concept for which communism is looking. Next, she turned to I John 4 and asked him to read verses 7 to 10, which state that love is from God. The man invited Christ into his life.

Before Miss Lee went to China, a friend from her church had given her the address of a relative, a high school teacher, living in the outskirts of Peking. On the way to visit him, her taxi was stopped by a policeman. The policeman asked her to call the teacher to inform him that she would not be able to meet him. She dialed twice, but both times the phone was busy.

She recalled how Peter, after seeing a vision from the Lord, had entered Cornelius' home. So, with this in mind, she prayed and stared at the policeman. A few minutes later the policeman told her she could go into the area.

When Miss Lee arrived at the school, the teacher was waiting for her. He took her to his home, and asked his wife to join them. Miss Lee shared the Four Spiritual Laws with the couple and both invited Christ into their hearts. On her way back to the hotel, Miss Lee also presented the gospel to the taxi driver. When they reached the hotel, he too invited Christ into his life.

Another day, Miss Lee tried to present the gospel to a group of young people in a park in Shanghai, but many of them laughed when she mentioned God. However, one man in his mid-20's did not laugh. As he was praying, a university student passed by and also wanted Miss Lee to share the booklet with him. She replied that it was late, and she needed to return to her hotel. The student went with her. Outside the hotel, he also asked Jesus to come into his life.

One afternoon, Miss Lee visited another park in Shanghai, but even after an hour, she was unable to tell anyone how to know

Christ. As she began to leave the park, she heard a woman reading aloud to herself in English. Miss Lee approached the woman, who was very happy to discover that she could speak English. The woman, who was in her 30's, worked as a translator in a nearby office.

After Miss Lee shared Christ with her, the woman received Christ into her life. She said, "I was waiting for someone like you. I am so glad you came." Miss Lee left the park at 5:20 p.m. and arrived at the hotel at 5:30 – just in time to leave for the next stop on her tour, Canton.

During her tour, Miss Lee talked with 50 peole about the claims of Christ. Of those, 26 professed to invite Christ to come into their lives. All but two were between the ages of 15 and 35.

"Many of the people I shared with were born during the communist regime," she said. "Despite the years of indoctrination, they were open to the gospel. All they needed was for someone to share with them and give them more pre-evangelistic information."

Since returning home, Miss Lee has received letters from 12 of those who indicated that they had invited Christ into their lives.

One of our staff members told me about a Chinese friend who lives in Los Angeles. After a 35-year absence, the Chinese man recently returned to China to visit his relatives for three weeks. There, he had the privilege of leading 13 members of his family, old and young, to Christ!

A Chinese church in Los Angeles has related that there are 15 foreign students from China who began to visit their church. Even though those who travel outside of China have been well indoctrinated, within six months eight of the students invited Christ into their lives and have been baptized.

I know of 11 pastors in China who are ministering among 118 house churches in one area. These house churches average 60 people each. This means 7,080 Christians in one small area of that vast country are meeting regularly for worship and fellowship.

Recently I heard a report directly from one worker in China. This worker said that the number of people attending house churches in one city had increased by 700 people between October and December, 1980.

Another beautiful story tells of a pastor who spent 19 years imprisoned for his faith in Christ. He is an artist and paints just enough to provide food for himself and his family as he ministers to 62 house churches. His son showed a friend of mine a letter he had received from his artist-pastor father many years ago while he was still in prison. "They advise me to repent and not believe in God," the father wrote, "but I will not agree. They can ask me to break my neck or shed my blood, but ask me not to believe in God – that's impossible!"

It is because of faith in God and the perseverance of men like this pastor that wonderful things are happening in China today. As courageous Christians in China pray and boldly share His message, the church will continue to grow and develop.

Illustrations of the immense hunger to know God personally have also come by way of response letters to our radio program, beamed twice daily into China. Our first letter, dated July 12, 1979, came from a young man in Fukien province. He wrote:

"How are you? I am so happy to listen to the messages that you are broadcasting. I have received Christ today. I invited Him to come and stay in my life. I like your programs very much. Would you please send me your program schedule, so I can continue to hear the Lord's words, begin my new life in Jesus Christ and be filled with the Holy Spirit.

"I also hope that you will often send me those materials. I really need your help and encouragement. Much appreciation. 'Lord, take control of the throne of my life. Make me the kind of person you want me to be. I pray in Jesus' name. Amen!'"

Another letter caused one of the hourly employees with our Chinese radio ministry in Hong Kong to jump for joy when it was received. When she had lived in Mainland China, she had been a co-worker with the person whose letter she was reading. Through listening to the "Here's Life" programs, that acquaintance had become a Christian and was writing for follow-up materials.

Another listener, effectively applying the training in evangelism which is a regular feature of the program, wrote, "I have received the booklets from you, and have already done everything you said in your letter. Also, I shared the Four Spiritual Laws with others and with all my classmates. They were as happy to hear about Christ as I was."

The church in China needs our continued prayers now as it has in the past. We know of the obvious needs – more Bibles, trained leaders, discipleship materials and literature. But, it is uncertain what additional help they need, want or can get, and how we can most effectively be involved.

One thing we know is that the church in China is an indigenous church and it plans to stay that way. Our help in reaching China for Christ must be what they *want*, not what those of us outside China may *think* they want.

Let's rejoice! God continues to do a mighty work in and through the church of China. We may not understand everything that is happening, and this new kind of Christian in China may hand us some surprises in their degree of patriotism and political viewpoint...but they love the Savior and they are grateful to Him for filling the vacuum in their lives. We can love, accept and pray for them, for they are our brothers and sisters in Christ.

CHAPTER EIGHT

New Life Came Through The Air

So shall My Word be that goeth forth out of my mouth. It shall not return unto me void, but it shall accomplish that which I please, and it shall prosper in the thing whereto I sent it.

Isaiah 55:11

A 23-year-old man sat in the small bare room called home. He was bored. And restless. His early shift at the factory caused late afternoon to run into a long evening. Of doing nothing. He felt there was more to life – a vague longing inside told him so. But he didn't know what it was. More education? A more challenging job? He didn't know. Anyway, neither was available to him.

Contemplating his immediate alternatives – to continue sitting in the bare room or to wander outside joining other uneasy young men with similar questions, who lingered on crowd-filled street corners – he began to turn the dial of his short wave radio. Listening to this small plastic box had become a habit with him. Through it he could learn about a world beyond his four walls, drown out his boredom and doubts with music, improve the English with which he struggled, or just while away his time.

The question he dreaded most drifted through his mind once more, "Is there a purpose to life?" Faintly from his radio, a catchy theme song and a title full of hope grabbed for his attention. The message stirred the emptiness within him. New life? Could there really be a light in this dark world?

That is a picture painted from the letters in our files. It is a make-believe story which happens to be true of millions of people who are now within reach of some of the most reassuring words ever spoken: "You can find new life in Jesus Christ!"

It doesn't take much imagination to realize that the following letter, actually received from somewhere in China a few months ago, could have been written in a small bare room called home.

"When I sent you my first letter six weeks ago, I had just accepted Jesus Christ as my Savior through tuning in to your radio program called 'Here's Life.' Before then, life to me was only a routine of eating, drinking and being merry. That is how I spent my time. I did think of religion, but could only wonder what to believe.

"Real life taught me that faith and truth were very hard to attain. For years, I have been like a lost sheep wandering on the crossroads looking for a Savior, the Lamp of life, the Light in darkness. Through the air, you have brought me the gospel of the Lord Jesus Christ and enabled me to have a share in God's supernatural love, peace and joy."

Campus Crusade for Christ originally ventured into a radio ministry for two reasons. First, radio waves can go where you and I will never go. They can enable us to get our training principles into China, North Korea and other places we cannot presently send staff members. Second, as we strategized regarding the "Jesus" film project and our plan to show this film everywhere in Asia, we felt that if we could begin broadcasting we would have an immediate follow-up vehicle directly tied to our ministry through which we could reach those in remote areas or in circumstances that prevented us from using normal follow-up strategies.

We faced many challenges in beginning this new ministry. Our research revealed that no one had ever attempted to air the type of training we wanted to produce. We were moving into an area where we could find no expertise. The staff assigned to this ministry were not experienced or knowledgeable in the field of broadcasting. So, this caused us to pray, and to pray much.

Also, through our research we discovered very few evangelistic radio programs in existence. Most Christian programming is either an inspirational message, a Bible study or music. This fact led us to develop a pre-evangelistic, an evangelistic and a discipleship training series.

A year and a half later, we began to air 90 programs grouped into three series of 30 half-hour training sessions. The first and second series includes Campus Crusade for Christ's Introductory and Intermediate training in evangelism and discipleship. The third series involves training sessions covering doctrinal issues. Written in English, these models were culturally adapted and translated into nine languages, and presently they are being broadcast into nine countries. This represents a potential listening audience of 1.5 billion people every day of the year. Each time the series is completed, it is simply aired again, so every three-months the cycle is repeated.

Our program, entitled "Here's Life," began in mid-1979 when Trans World Radio beamed our first 30-minute broadcast into China. Through their facilities located on Guam, twice each day – in the morning and in the evening – listeners on the Chinese mainland can take the same training we conduct in countries all over the world. Since 1979 we have launched daily programs into Burma, Bangladesh, Indonesia, India (in Hindi and Bengali languages), Korea, Nepal, Philippines and Thailand. Besides the facilities of Trans World Radio, we also use those of Far East Broadcasting Company as well as two government-owned stations.

It is difficult to determine the actual ministry that a radio program has, especially when it goes into countries where we have little or no access to the people. Since beams are randomly shot through the air with a prayer that they are heard, the most effective way we have to determine results of a broadcast is through response letters. We are told that in the United States every letter represents 1,000 listeners. In Asia we know the representation would be much higher but we do not know how much higher.

In Burma, for example, during 1980 we received 2,344 letters. In those letters 412 people stated that they had invited Christ into their lives. An additional 328 stated that they had prayed to be filled with the Holy Spirit by faith, and 317 signed up for training in evangelism and discipleship.

In the remaining pages of this chapter, I want to share with you excerpts from letters received in our radio response and follow-up centers across Asia. Since they fall easily into several major categories, I have grouped them accordingly. As you read the letters, please remember that they are translated into English from nine different Asian languages.

I. CHRISTIAN LITERATURE

As Christians, we often have a tendency to take certain things for granted. Christian literature is one of these. How easy it is to discard a booklet because it has become old or soiled. How many Bibles, in how many translations, do we find lining our personal library shelves. But, how precious Christian literature becomes when you have *none.*

The following letters come from China.

"I was very happy to receive your letter dated July 29, and the enclosed booklet, 'How to Be Sure You Are a Christian.' Thank you. I have checked on the Bibles that you sent, but to no avail. What a pity! Is it that the Bible is forbidden? If that is so, then please do not waste any more of your effort. Yet, the Bible is what I need to further understand the Lord Jesus Christ. May I request that you try having the Bible sent by registered mail? Hope to hear from you soon."

"I am a high school student, and for a long time I have been listening to your station. The programs have been very helpful and have taught me great lessons. I believe in God and I am a Christian, yet without a Bible it will not be possible for me to know God well or to hear Him speak. In our place, it is impossible for us to purchase Bibles. This is why I am hoping that you will send me one. I will be waiting at home for your reply. May my Lord grant us protection and success in our undertaking. Amen!"

"My friend shared with me the booklet, 'Have You Heard of the Four Spiritual Laws?' that you sent him. I found it very helpful and would like to have more literature of the kind. From the back page of the booklet, I learned that you have a Bible study series and other helpful material for Christian growth and witness. I would like to have some of those, like 'How To Be Sure You Are A Christian.' Please be concerned enough to send them to me."

"Thank God! I received your reply and the Christian booklets. I am grateful for your concern. The two Transferable Concept booklets have been very helpful. Do continue to send me booklets like these so that I may grow spiritually and be God's useful vessel."

"Brothers and sisters in Campus Crusade for Christ, we have begun our weekly worship service this year, but many of us do not have the Bible. After reading this letter, I hope you can send us more than a hundred copies."

"Right now, I'm studying for my exams, but still cannot help writing you because I want the booklet on 'How to Pray.' I've been a Christian for many years but don't know how to pray."

"I hope my letter will reach your hand safely through God's power. Praise the Lord that we can correspond. I am a new Christian and recently I obtained a New Testament. My wish is to have the Old Testament also. I wonder if you can help me in this. This morning's radio message, 'How to Witness in the Spirit,' Booklet 15, if available can I have one? Also please send me a copy of the Four Spiritual Laws."

"I received your letter and the Bible. Due to my busy schedule, I have delayed the reply until today. Thank you for sending me the booklets and the Bible. With the teaching and revelation of the Holy Spirit, these will be used to help us grow in the abundant life of Christ."

"How are you? I have received your reply and the booklets 'How to Be Sure You are a Christian' and 'Beginning Your New Life in Christ.' I have read the booklets and they have been very helpful in my getting to know the Savior, Jesus Christ. Thank you very much for your help and encouragement."

II. INDIVIDUALS ACCEPTING CHRIST

The greatest blessing is to read letters from people who receive Christ by faith. The Scriptures tell us that the angels rejoice when one comes to know Him personally. I often have the great privilege of rejoicing with the angels as I read letters like these.

From Korea:

"I am a 50-year-old working woman. When I heard about the basic steps towards Christian maturity, I decided to believe on Christ."

"I am 50 years old. I listen to your radio program, and I prayed to God for assurance and salvation."

"I received Christ by listening to your program."

"I received Christ and I have assurance of salvation. I now practice Christian fellowship with other believers."

From China:

"It was just recently that I, as a listener, heard your warm voice from the transistor radio. The Here's Life program is well presented in content and arrangement. I am very impressed. You know what? I have accepted the New Life! Christ has granted me the strength to work and to study."

"Today, I received Christ!! Please, I am asking you for a special favor to send me Booklet 7. Wishing you happiness and smooth work."

"I received Jesus Christ today as I had the opportunity to understand the secrets of the gospel and the Four Spiritual Laws. To help my listening of the future programs I would like to have the booklet written by Dr. Bright."

From Malaysia:

"One night as I was tuning and listening to a radio broadcast, suddenly I heard the Lord's call which enabled me, a sinner, to gain new life. I want to be a child of God, to have all my sins cleansed, to have eternal life, so, I asked God to live in my life forever."

From Thailand:

"On August 11, 1980 I listened to the radio program for the first time. I was touched that God loves me because I have never known anyone who would love me and help me. As a result, I listened to the program again on August 18 and then I made the decision to receive Jesus."

III. REQUESTS FOR MORE INFORMATION ABOUT CHRIST

There are those who are genuinely seeking answers in life. They have valid questions about how they can establish a personal relationship with Christ.

"How are you? I am your regular listener and I like your Here's Life program very much. I would like to accept Jesus Christ as my Savior, but I have not had enough information. To help me in my understanding of a personal relationship with Jesus Christ, please send me 'How to Be Sure You Are a Christian' and other Christian literature. I have requested a Bible, but have not received it yet."

"I am very happy to have received your letter. I am very anxious to understand the belief of Christianity, so I am asking you to send me a Bible. I believe the Bible will be able to answer my questions."

"I am an atheist, and I do not believe that heaven and earth were created by God! Today, listening to Here's Life broadcast on love, it illumined me a little. Can you please send me additional information?"

"How are you? I am your regular listener. Your Here's Life programs have been among my favorites. I desire very much to receive Jesus Christ as the Lord of my life. I wish I could have some Bible study guides on Jesus Christ. Can you please help me?"

IV. A HUNGER REVEALED AMONG OTHER RELIGIONS

Following the first two broadcasts to India in the Hindi language, 14 letters were received within three days. All the letters were from Hindus and all 14 writers stated that they had received Christ. Excerpts from several of these letters follows:

From Hindus in India:

"I heard your radio program and I was very much impressed to hear about how I can become a Christian. Now that I have become a Christian, I would like to learn more about the Holy Spirit."

"By hearing your radio program I came to learn more about Jesus Christ and accepted Him as my personal Savior."

"I have accepted the Lord Jesus Christ as my personal Savior and I am experiencing Him in my daily life."

"As a result of hearing your program my curiosity grew in my heart to know more about Jesus Christ, and I am trusting Him as my Savior."

From a Muslim in India:

"Your program is very fine. Though I was born a Muslim, now I believe on the Lord Jesus Christ. Thank you for helping me to know Him personally."

From Korea:

"I was born in a family with a strict Confucian backgroud. But, through listening to your program, Christ became the Savior of my soul."

V. HOW TO BE FILLED WITH THE HOLY SPIRIT

Training people in how to be filled with the Holy Spirit sets believers on a course toward victorious Christian living.

From Burma:

"I am writing my first letter to you with an exceeding joyful spirit. Ever since I first learned about your station, no matter how busy I might be, I always make time to listen. It has been our precious opportunity to learn from you concerning the Lord's work and the Bible. We have been greatly encouraged to seek the truth, and to strive for spiritual growth.

"Though I have been a Christian form some time I have just learned about carnality. Sometimes in satisfying my own desires I forget about God's will. Please pray for me. Whenever I tune in to your program, I always have my pen ready and I listen attentively. Thank you for your hard work that has enabled me to handle temptation and troubles through trusting the Holy Spirit to control me."

From Indonesia:

"Please forgive me if I have written your name wrongly. Let me first express my respect to all of your broadcasting personnel. I thank the Lord for leading me to tune in to the Here's Life program, conducted by you with your articulate voice. It has been very helpful to me because the filling of the Holy Spirit has changed me from a carnal to a spiritual Christian."

"Hello! I heard your Here's Life program tonight. It made me realize how I can live a victorious Christian life and how a Christian can draw life from Christ."

From Malaysia:

"The Here's Life program today talked about the spiritual and carnal lives of Christians. There were times when I found reading the Bible very interesting and my prayer life was serene and sweet. Yet, most of the time I found myself living the carnal life you described. Prayer did not seem important, I did not read the Bible, my life was fruitless and miserable.

"There was no peace and joy in my heart. Oh, how I hate that kind of life! I struggled and tried hard to change it, but my effort was in vain. The Here's Life program tonight certainly helped me. I believe that with the help you offered, I can be changed from a carnal to a spiritual Christian."

From China:

"Your radio program is very profitable for my spiritual growth. Thank you for providing me those books which explain how I can continually walk with the Lord and experience a full and abundant life."

From India:

"After praying with you, I feel very peaceful and I was filled with the Spirit. Since being filled with the Spirit is the command of God, what I need to do is to obey the command, claim His promise and live by faith, allowing God to take control my life. Then, I shall be filled with the spirit forever."

"At the time when I was not growing spiritually, you taught me how to grow in the Christian life through your radio program. I am thankful to you for that. May the Lord help this program and help those who are in need of spiritual growth."

VI. TRAINING IN HOW TO SHARE CHRIST WITH OTHERS

When trained in how to live the abundant Christian life and how to share Christ with others, believers begin to multiply spiritually.

From Korea:

"I thank God, that through your program I am receiving many benefits in my Christian life. I am learning to share my faith with those who do not know Christ."

"As I listen to the program, my love for souls increased. I am now dedicated to sharing Christ with everyone."

"The program has helped me to gain two disciples. This became possible through your radio training."

From Burma:

"Recently, I heard you talk about using the Four Spiritual Laws in drawing people to Christ. The content is practical and precise, and is exactly what I need. I have been a Christian for many years. However, my lack of growth spiritually has disabled me to be of use to the Lord. Yet, having received the Lord's abundant grace, it is my desire to witness for Him that my life may be more meaningful."

From China:

"The Here's Life program has been very helpful to us in living the victorious Christian life. Knowing that the Great Commission was given by the Lord has enabled me to see that every Christian bears a very important responsibility. We cannot afford to spend our days leisurely. Rather, we should diligently accomplish the commission that our Lord Jesus Christ gave to every believer so that this Great Commission may be accomplished sooner. This is His command."

From India:

"I was asking the Lord to teach me how to tell others about Him. As an answer to my prayer you have explained it through your evening radio program. Praise God that I can use that method in bringing others to the Lord."

Miracles in the Air

One of the many miracles which God has performed enables us to braodcast our Here's Life radio programs into the high Himalayan mountains of Nepal. In late 1979 while visiting with our staff in Nepal we were disucssing our plans for 1980. We felt that radio was desperately needed, but because of the high mountains and the location of the Christian radio stations in Asia they were unable to get a clear signal into Nepal.

The laws of Nepal forbid anyone to convert to Christianity, so I knew it would not be permissible to use local stations. I inquired of our director which stations from outside the country came in clearly.

He replied that there is only one reliable station – Radio Sri Lanka. My heart sank, for I knew it would be impossible to receive approval from a government radio company in one Buddhist country to broadcast the gospel into another country where Buddhism is one of the predominant religions. Nevertheless, we prayed together asking God to work out the situation for His glory.

The following week, while in India with our mass media director for Asia, we discussed the situation in Nepal. When I asked him to go to Sri Lanka regarding this matter, he presented me with the same objections I had raised. Again, we prayed, committing the matter to the Lord.

Our mass media director went to Sri Lanka the following week and met with the Radio Sri Lanka personnel to ask about the possibility of buying radio time in order to beam our program to Nepal. They promptly said **no**!

However, that same evening while at a dinner party he met a friend associated with our ministry who is in the film industry. Our director explained to his friend what we were trying to do and asked if she had any suggestions. She immediately went to the telephone and called the managing director of the government station, who is a Buddhist. Through this telephone call, arrangements were made. The next morning our mass media director returned to the Radio Sri Lanka station. Within one hour he was signing a contract which would enable us to broadcast our program into Nepal.

It is a miracle for one Buddhist country to broadcast the gospel into another, but that is exactly what happens seven days a week throughout the year. Thus far, out of 1,000 letters received, 354 Nepalese have written to say that they received Christ after hearing His message via Radio Sri Lanka.

VII. ENCOURAGEMENT

The final category of letters received brings constant cheer to us and motivates us to continue trusting God for even greater miracles in the air. They are described with one word: encouragement!

"I am a Trans World old-time listener in China. I have been using your Here's Life programs in encouraging other brothers and sisters. It also has been very helpful to me in my own spiritual growth. Your program, which is after 9 p.m., has been like a rich spiritual feast to me. On behalf of my brother, sisters and relatives, may I express my gratitude to you. In the coming year, may the Lord keep you, add unto you grace and give you strength, that you may love the Lord even deeper."

"Even with my busy schedule, I will still turn on my precious transistor radio to listen to your training program with full attention. Your language is plain and good, easy to understand and attractive. Thank you for your friendly service through the air. Thank you for having helped us, your faithful listeners (including me), with our problems."

"I am from Guantong province. May I, on behalf of all your faithful listeners, express my gratitude to you. What I need now are the training lesson plans, Christian manual and other related materials."

"I have been wanting to write you, but because of other considerations I have been hesitant. I received Christ a long time ago, yet I still have no Bible. I hope you could send me one and other related books, so that I may learn more about our wonderful Savior. Tonight is Christmas night. Remembering the abundant grace of our Lord has encouraged me to boldly pick up the pen and write to you."

PART III
Church Growth

CHAPTER NINE

Awakening Leads To Church Growth

"You are wasting your time to send your staff to that Buddhist village. No one there has received Christ in more than 38 years!"

These were the "encouraging" words one of our village staff teams heard before they entered a particular village in Northeast Thailand. However, because their goal was to saturate *every* village in their assigned area with the claims of Christ, they asked God for boldness. Then they set out to give even these reportedly hardened Buddhist villagers the opportunity to respond to new life in Jesus.

Leaving the results to God, they began sharing their faith and contacting village leaders, making preparation to show the "Jesus" film. Four days later more than 50 people had indicated positive decisions for Christ. One of those was the leader of the village. Before the team departed, a church, or home fellowship, had already begun to meet in this leader's home.

These people were not hardened to the gospel at all. They were only assumed by many to be hardened. Actually, these villagers knew nothing about God's love and forgiveness, so there was a very logical reason why no one had received Christ in 38 years. They had not heard or understood His message!

Thirty-three New Churches Overnight

In Thailand, over a six-month period of time, our ministry had the opporutnity to train 293 village workers. They were individuals who had committed one year to help reach their country with the claims of Christ. Their 30-day training session in evangelism and discipleship was short but intense. Then they divided into 23 teams.

After three months of laboring in the whitened fields of Thailand, these village staff workers had exposed more than 150,000 people to the claims of Christ. More than 50,000 people indicated decisions for Christ. Thirty-three new house churches so the new believers could worship and fellowship together.

These Thai village workers are among thousands of people across Asia who have been raised up by God and are highly committed to help reach their countries for Christ. During their training, the village workers are told that if God provides the funds, they will receive a minimal living allowance and nothing more. Even this does not alter their determination to serve Christ in this way.

One volunteer was a 79-year-old pastor who underwent our intensive training. This month-long training equipped him to have a personal ministry of winning and building others for Christ. He stated that he had never expereienced this type of training before.

His age was not this elderly gentleman's only unique qualification. He was also a multiplier. He brought his son, his grandson and his great-grandson to undergo training with him. All four generations have committed themselves to be village workers with Thailand's rural outreach strategy.

For two months, these village workers and others like them worked without a living allowance because the money was simply not available. However, because of their commitment they continued to minister by faith. Often they had no money for food or transportation, yet God unfailingly met their needs.

In many cases, the people of completely pagan villages were so happy that the workers had come to share Christ in their village that they housed and fed them and even supplied transportation to the next village on their circuit. Shaking his head in amazement, one director remarked, "My 'Jesus' film team workers were getting fat and they had no money!"

Rural churches are springing up all across Asia. In order for these baby churches to have mature leadership, denominations are being encouraged to work with our village teams and accept the responsibility for nurturing these new believers.

The large majority of the areas in which the village teams travel are without churches. In these areas, it is delightful to observe small house churches being born and starting to grow overnight. These new believers themselves see the need for a church to be established in their area after receiving our basic follow-up instruction.

In India, during 1980, 1,134 pastors underwent this same kind of concentrated evangelism and discipleship training. Soon they began to see their churches grow, and they are realizing their dream of opening daughter churches as additional people are responding to the gospel.

One 600-member church in Madras, India, underwent several Campus Crusade for Christ lay training seminars. Within three months, after 40% of its members began to witness regularly, this church had increased by 25%.

People are hungry for the gospel. When they hear, many respond. For more than 25 years, Dr. Bill Bright has repeatedly made the statement that "people are standing in line to hear about Christ." This statement remains true today. As Christians share Christ by faith, responsive people are there to listen. Sharing in Muslim areas is more difficult, but even they are open to His promise of new life.

A Muslim layman said, "I am a Muslim by faith. After reading your booklet 'I found it! You can find it too!' I believe Christ is the only way for salvation. I invited Him into my life. Please tell me what I should do from now on."

A Muslim professor wrote, "The testimonies of the young people in your 'I found it!' paper touched me and I would like to know Christ. Please help me."

A Muslim college student rejoiced, "Through your booklet I found new life in Jesus Christ! I would like to share my joy with you. Please guide me."

These people and thousands like them are newborn Christians asking for our help. We know they *need* to grow; they know they *desire* to grow.

The three nations in the world with the largest Muslim

populations are in Asia. Often, village film teams have literally taken their lives into their hands when going into all-Muslim villages with the Christian film, "Jesus." In spite of this, in one of these countries, 40,000 Muslims saw the "Jesus" film in their own villages within two months.

Collecting response cards is impossible in many of these places, because Muslims face great danger in admitting they are interested in Christ. To overcome this problem, film teams have begun distributing postcards which can be mailed secretly. Upon receiving these postcards, leaders then send back replies to the inquirers in a plain envelope to protect these new Christians.

One church in a strongly Muslim village had a regular attendance of only 14 people. Two weeks after the film, "Jesus," had been shown in the village, attendance had grown to 60. Similar growth occurred in four churches in that area.

It is not easy to become a Christian in certain situations. In many countries new believers face a type of persecution most of us know nothing about.

For example, in Mandalay, Burma, five Buddhist students became Christians within two weeks of one another. Because their lives were changed after receiving Christ, these young girls shared with their parents that they had become Christians. Their parents became very bitter. One daughter was taken to the village temple and beaten before the monks and the people worshipping there.

The other four girls endured similar treatment. After their beatings all five said, "Praise the Lord. By His grace we were able to bear it." They would not reject Christ, and have now joined a local church.

In other situations when the gospel is presented, the individual may experience no opposition, but the result is the same—the heart is responsive, the life is changed and growth begins.

In Okinawa, Japan, during our mass media campaign, a 10-year-old boy sat watching television. For several days "I found it!" was flashed before his eyes repeatedly. His curiousity aroused many times the little boy asked his parents what "I found it!" meant, but they were unable to tell him.

When the reveal portion proclaimed on his screen, "I found it! You can find it too! New Life in Christ!" he quickly memorized the telephone number listed and dashed to the phone to satisfy his curiosity. Later that day a couple was assigned to visit the young boy. They were hoping to involve him in their Sunday school program. Upon arriving in his home, the couple explained the gospel to him through the Four Spiritual Laws and he asked Christ into his life. He assured them that he would begin attending Sunday school.

His mother had been listening to their conversation. Politely she asked the couple, "Would you mind sharing the same thing with me?" Again, they went through the Four Spiritual Laws booklet, this time with the mother, and she too received Christ by faith.

By this time, the boy's father, who is the president of a large construction company, had come home. For the third time, the couple shared the message contained in this small booklet and the father also professed faith in Christ. Because of this little boy's inquisitiveness, his whole family was awakened to their need of a Savior. Now this family is well established in a church, has been baptized and hosts a weekly Bible study in their home.

Far into the mountains of the Philippines, one of our staff men drove with a pastor to a small municipality in Isabela to a small *barrio* where our Campus Crusade ministry had never been. There they came to a little *nipa*-hut church.

Entering the church, they discovered 140 children sitting on the dirt floor. In the center of the room a teacher had a little chalkboard upon which she had drawn two circles. As she explained to the children that these two circles represented two kinds of lives, they followed along with Four Spiritual Laws fliers in the Ilocano language. Amazed, our staff member waited until the conclusion of her session to find out how she had learned to make this presentation that he had personally given hundreds of time before.

He discovered that she had attended a teacher's conference for Daily Vacation Bible School workers in a different municipality where one of our Campus Crusade village staff members had been invited to speak. The staff member had conducted our basic seminars on "How To Witness." Then, he had given each participant a supply of Four Spiritual Laws fliers for use in his own *barrio*.

This woman had then taken them back to her bamboo church in the mountains and was using them to share Christ with the children of her village.

Trekking at 13,000 Feet

The letter before me read, "Our village workers are now trekking at 13,000 feet!" Immediately I knew the significance of that statement.

As the Nepalese say, "Nepal is at the top of the world." Located in the midst of the Himalayan mountains, it boasts the tallest mountain in the world, Mt. Everest. Much of the country is mountainous and inaccessible by road. One must trek over hills and through valleys to get from one town to another.

The letter I received indicated that the 1980 saturation program in Nepal, named "Target 80," was just about completed. Our director was rejoicing, and as I read I too rejoiced because I knew the significance of climbing to 13,000 feet in that small Himalayan kingdom. Generally, people do not live above 13,000 feet!

In 1975, when our director returned to Nepal following eight months of training in our Great Commission Training Center in Manila, there were 400 to 500 baptized Christians in his country. Nepal is a country closed to Christianity. It is illegal for a person to preach or share his faith in public. The law prohibits a person changing from one religion to another. Yet the constitution states that there is religious freedom in Nepal!

This is the atmosphere in which our director had been raised, and to which he had to return. When he had left his country for Manila he was just an average Christian–one of the 400 to 500 baptized believers. When he returned he had a vision to see his country reached for Christ, and he knew he had a workable plan to do it.

In Manila, he had been instructed to simply go back and apply his training in his own situation. He did just that. As he began to go out witnessing each day, he discovered that the people of his country were responsive to the gospel. Soon he decided to conduct evangelistic meetings as he had been trained to do. During his first meeting, 150 students were present and more than 50 indicated they had received Christ into their lives.

This increased his confidence that God could work in the hearts of his people. So, in spite of his situation, he began to train a few Christians in how to share Christ with others. The results of these training sessions were rewarding, even though some ended up spending time in jail because they applied their training.

The history of Christianity shows that persecution brings boldness to believers. It certainly did in Nepal. Christians became willing to go to jail for Christ, if that was required to reach others with His message.

The mobilization of the Nepalese church began with these small training sessions. Soon believers were taking the gospel to the remotest corners of their nation. The Holy Spirit was working in a wonderful way, and by the end of 1979 there were 8,000 baptized Christians in Nepal!

Our director's vision to see his country saturated with the gospel became infectious. When he shared his strategy with church leaders, they became enthusiastic and gave their wholehearted support to his strategy for evangelizing Nepal. Two hundred and thirty-two church fellowships united together with the major Christian organizations and missions ministering in Nepal, and "Target 80" became the nationwide goal of every Christian.

The principle objectives of "Target 80" were to distribute evangelistic literature across Nepal, to encourage people to listen to our "Here's Life" radio program, to show the film, "Jesus," and to motivate every individual Christian to share the gospel with at least two people each day.

For the first time in the history of Nepal, every church throughout the country began 24-hour prayer chains. All the Christians of Nepal joined a 168-hour prayer chain. One hundred prayer cells were formed to pray specifically for "Target 80."

Nepal Christian Fellowship arranged four large conferences in which Nepal Campus Crusade for Christ conducted evangelistic and discipleship training from October 12-18, 1980. A total of 5,000 people attended these conferences. Following their training, the participants returned to their homes with as many pieces of literature as they needed to saturate every home in their area.

With each person giving at least 30 days of involvement in this 80-day literature distribution program, 945 Christians spread across Nepal to place literature in every possible home in the country. They were grouped into 47 geographic teams. These teams trekked throughout the mountains from October 19 to December 31, 1980, distributing 1,600,000 newsprint copies of a specially-designed Four Spiritual Laws flier. An additional 122 people from various churches were trained in how to conduct basic follow-up classes, and they were also assigned to follow the literature distribution teams.

To assist in this overall strategy to win and disciple Nepalese for Christ, the film, "Jesus," played a unique role. Among Buddhists, Hindus and Communists, it is used to change their thinking about who Jesus is. For the first time, many formed positive concepts about Jesus and Christianity.

"Target 80" proved to be a renewing and reviving force for the Christians of Nepal. Almost every believer in Nepal shared the claims of Christ with at least two people eacy day. As the believers began to experience the power of the Holy Spirit in their lives, the momentum increased and they began to trust God for even bigger things.

As a result, all Christian churches and organizations were united in one goal – to help fulfill the Great Commission in Nepal during 1980. They experienced great boldness as they worked toward this goal. Due to their efforts, 80% of the country was exposed to the name of Jesus. Twenty-five percent heard a clear presentation of the gospel. For most, this was the first time they had heard that Jesus in the *only* way to God.

Now you, too, can understand the significance of trekking at 13,000 feet! What rejoicing must have taken place as these daring, persistent Christians, most of whom were probably less than five years old in the Lord, realized that the gospel message had gone into every area and almost every home of the country located on top of the world.

This did not happen without trials and persecution. These believers ran great risks as they committed themselves to this challenging task to go to cities, villages and remote areas of the Himalayas. Forty-six people were arrested for sharing the gospel. Three months later three were still in jail. But even with that kind of pressure, the movement did not stop. One staff volunteer was arrested three times in 80 days. This joyfully obedient Christian said, "It was a great joy for me to share the love of Christ to the people on the inside of the jail!"

The first phase of "Target 80" has been completed, but the momentum continues. As Christians remain faithful to share the beautiful message of Christ, the Nepal church continues to grow. "Target 80" is just the beginning of a movement which will continue reaching people until the second coming of Jesus Christ, declares our Nepal director.

In 1975, there were 400 to 500 baptized Christians in Nepal. In 1979 there were 8,000. By the end of 1980 there were 15,000 baptized believers – and the church continues to grow every day.

It should be pointed out that in 1980, 49,266 people indicated decisions for Jesus Christ through the various Nepal Campus Crusade for Christ strategies. In Nepal, these people are referred to as believer-Christians. Experience has proven that most overcome the fear of persecution as they are discipled. As their faith grows they become baptized Christians in the church of Nepal.

Light a spark in a forest and it becomes a forest fire. Plant a fireseed in the jungles of Thailand or the mountains of Nepal and it will produce an awakening. An awakening leads to growth in the lives of individuals and in the life of the local church.

CHAPTER TEN

Training Makes The Difference

"Dear Sir,

I am the pastor of a young congregation which was founded four years ago in Surabaya, Indonesia. We believe the Lord will bless our church, and He has! For our first step, we determined a faith target of erecting a church building that would accommodate 250. The second step was a building for 1,000. The third step is a building for 5,000. The first step has already been completed. For the second step, we dedicated a building for 1,000 on September 29, 1980.

"When Here's Life, Surabaya preparation began in our church, we occupied the building that could accommodate 250 persons. We assigned 19 members to go through the training course on evangelism and discipleship. We experienced tremendous results! Our 250 members doubled. Now 500 people attend our Sunday morning service. The record number who worshipped in our church in 1980 is 800. During that year, 329 were baptized. I would like to say that this is the result of our joint ministry with Here's Life.

"We plan to send 40 members to attend the four-month training course at the Here's Life Center. All expenses during their training will be paid by us. We are convinced we will have positive results because of the ministries of the 19 members who joined your basic training on evangelism and discipleship. They multiplied the number of people attending our Sunday service last year from 250 to 500. We believe, by December, 1981, that number will be multiplied by 1,000.

"If, by the end of this year, we see our third step of reaching the target of 5,000 attendance accomplished, we would like to promote our joint-ministry with Indonesia Campus Crusade for Christ.

"It is worth relating in this testimony that, in addition to the foregoing, as the result of joining the Here's Life, Surabaya campaign, we have begun a weekly service for new believers in another part of Surabaya. This is a branch of our church. Glory be to our blessed Lord!

Alex Tanusaputra, Pastor
Bethel Church of Indonesia
Manyar Sindaru, Surabaya
Indonesia"

When Jesus Christ is lifted up by Spirit-filled Christians who are involved in evangelism and discipleship, great spiritual blessing comes to the organized church. The rate the church grows is not determined by man, but is determined by the Lord. However, we can be sure that when Christians are fulfilling their responsibilities, both quantitative and qualitative results will occur in the local church.

Four months after Here's Life, Korea and the '80 World Evangelization Crusade, our staff surveyed 64 churches in 16 districts. The information they discovered was staggering. The Korean church has experienced steady growth for many years, but following Campus Crusade for Christ's Explo '74 the growth rate tripled. It appears that, once again, it is increasing rapidly. In these 64 churches, church attendance has increased by an average of 38.8% since July, 1980, when Here's Life, Korea-'80 World Evangelization Crusade began.

The greatest increase was in the Pusan area where the attendance in two Presbyterian churches had increased 100% or more. One of these churches had an attendance of 200 in July and 450 in December. The other went from 350 to 700. Also, another church increased in attendance from 700 to 1,200 in the same six-month period of time.

Naturally, the churches with very large membership showed a lower percent but were also included in the survey. A Methodist church in Inchon showed a 33% increase when a 4,000 attendance in July increased to 5,000 in December. The largest church in the world, The Full Gospel Central Church in Seoul, experiences a constant increase in membership. In those same six months, its membership rose to 11% which is several percentage points above its normal increase, going from 131,940 to 147,011 members.

Other countries also experienced remarkable church growth during 1980. Trained members from one small church in the western Visayas region of the Philippines followed up contacts who had professed to invite Christ into their lives during the simultaneous Here's Life campaign and Operation Jabez. Within 20 days, that church had baptized 74 new church members.

Following their participation with an Operation Jabez team in Isulan, another small Filipino church reported that they had 130 first-time attenders in their morning worship service within two Sundays after the OJ team had left their area.

In 1978 six churches were involved in Here's Life, Macau. In 1980 there were 12 churches participating in Macau's Saturation '80. Five of the additional six churches had been established since 1978 as a direct result of Here's Life, Macau. Before 1978, Macau was considered by most denominations to be a barren place to minister. The churches that existed did not have fulltime pastors. Now, the situation is changing. Five denominations from Hong Kong purchased property in Macau last year and are now planning to locate churches there.

In many locations the rate of church growth is not always this positive. However, we can always be assured that when we take the responsibility seriously to go out and tell people about His Son, God will take care of the results, whether they are visible or not.

Okinawa, Japan is one such place. As stated earlier, Here's Life, Okinawa resulted in 1,800 decisions for Christ. Yet, the church has grown very little in either attendance or membership. It is interesting to note, however, that of the 1,800 who indicated decisions to accept Christ, 700 are still attending home Bible studies. This is the highest percentage of attendance in any city across Asia which held a Here's Life campaign.

Dr. Billy Graham held evangelistic crusades in five cities in Japan in 1980. The successful Tokyo crusade drew the largest Christian gathering ever held in that city. There was a total attendance of 130,000 in five days, 11,000 decisions for Christ were indicated. Tokyo's population is 12 million people.

Okinawa has a population of one million people. The Okinawa Billy Graham Crusade drew a total attendance of 33,000 in only two days and there were 5,000 professions of faith. This means that 15% of those in attendance indicated decisions for Christ. This is a very high percentage of responses for Japan, and a much higher percentage than indicated in Japan's other four crusade cities.

Because of Here's Life, Okinawa the Christians had been thoroughly trained in evangelism and discipleship. They also had a vision to see all of Okinawa reached for Christ and were mobilized to accomplish that goal, and these were factors contributing to the success of Bill Graham's crusade. Another factor in the response to Graham's crusade was the media campaign of Here's Life. Following a Here's Life campaign in a city, the non-Christian population experiences an awareness of God which is impossible to measure, but which causes people to be responsive to the gospel.

The church in Okinawa has begun to spread its roots throughout Okinawan society, even though it is not experiencing an obvious increase in attendance. For example, the Kin Baptist Church trained 20 of its 38 members during the campaign. These 20 introduced 120 people to Christ in two months. Before the Here's Life campaign, this church had practically no non-Christian contacts outside the church. Though actual church attendance has not increased, they now have at least 700 neighborhood contacts to whom their members minister regularly. This same church chartered 12 buses to take more than 500 people to the Billy Graham Crusade.

Here's Life, Taiwan (ROC), which began in 1977, is continuing because churches across the country are united with the common goal of confronting everyone in the country with the claims of Christ. As the people who are won to Christ are discipled, these churches are growing.

As an outgrowth of their Here's Life campaign in August, 1980, 300 Taiwan churches across the island united for a week of personal evangelism and simultaneous evangelistic meetings. The meetings were held for five nights with an average attendance of 200 people in each church. There was a total attendance during the week of more than 300,000 people.

Training Made A Difference

"Training makes the difference" is one of the many mottoes of our movement. I have personally heard hundreds of testimonies from pastors all across Asia and the Pacific islands state that even with their many previous years of training, as thorough as their education may have been, they have never been trained effectively in personal evangelism and the "how to's" of basic follow-up and discipleship.

The church growth experiences of Bishop Sam Ponniah of the Church of South India in Vellore, India, are related in a previous chapter. Bishop Ponniah very freely says that for most of his years of ministry he had the desire to evangelize his entire diocese, but he did not know how to do it. Therefore, he was unable to train his pastors to do the job he felt needed to be done. Then the staff of India Campus Crusade for Christ came to him offering a strategy and a basic training course in evangelism and discipleship. At his request, our staff trained his pastors and church leaders. In turn, these leaders took our mediated training units and trained their own people.

Later an article appeared in one of our international publications stating that Bishop Ponniah had baptized more than 6,000 people. An acquaintance of his in the United States doubted the validity of the article and wrote the Bishop a letter, inquiring about it. The Bishop replied to his letter, stating, "You are correct. The article is not accurate – for I have now baptized more than 8,000 people!" And now, he has baptized 10,000. Bishop Ponniah's diocese is being evangelized and his church is growing.

A similar story could be told of Bishop Daniel Abraham in Tirunelveli, India, and also of the Church of South India. Phenomenal things have taken place in his church as a result of Spirit-filled men and women being trained and then taking seriously God's command to go and reach others with the gospel.

"... The harvest is plentiful, but the workers are few..." reflects the reality of Asia. In most countries fewer than one percent of the people are Christians. In almost all of our evangelistic thrusts, more people respond to the gospel that we are able to follow up in traditional one-to-one or small group methods.

In many cases, a few hundred Christians have thousands of contacts to follow up. As we anticipate proclaiming Christ on an even wider scale in the 1980's through the use of Here's Life, films, radio, village strategies and our campus ministry, the problem of discipling new believers becomes even greater.

The Here's Life Center, a relatively new ministry of discipleship for Campus Crusade for Christ, seeks to help meet this need. Although utilizing the same training in evangelism and discipleship already being offered through our other ministries, its objectives are: (1) to serve as a training resource for pastors and laymen in personal evangelism, and personal and group follow-up, and (2) to help follow up those contacts who are beyond the immediate reach of the churches, by offering classes for new Christians and opportunities for small group discipleship. The Here's Life Center staff in each city will build these new believers to the point of commitment to an existing local church, or they will help existing local churches or mission groups form new churches with these contacts.

The goal of our ministry is to establish at least one Here's Life Center in every city with a population of 50,000 or more. These Centers will also be located in rural areas where there are few Christians and few churches, but where large numbers of follow up contacts already exist, or are expected to be produced as a result of Here's Life strategies and our radio ministry.

Through a Here's Life Center already operating in Papau New Guinea, 30 pastors and church evangelists received our evangelism and discipleship training. As a result, thousands of lives are being reached for Christ through their ministry.

An evangelist with the United Church in Papua attended this training session. As soon as he was outfitted with his mediated training unit and equipped to train others, he returned to the circuit which had been assigned to him by his church. He trained almost every Christian in all the villages of his circuit. Those Christians shared Christ with more than 10,000 people. That year in his circuit alone more than 800 people were baptized.

Trained pastors in the Micronesia area of the Pacific have begun translating all of the training materials into the local languages at their own expense, so they can begin to train people of the smaller language groups.

The Here's Life Centers in Southern Mindanao, Philippines, have had more than 100 pastors and church leaders set aside two days each week from their schedules to receive training for three months. They travel to strategically located centers each week from surrounding areas and then return to their churches to apply what they have learned.

Every pastor who has taken the training and begun to apply it in his church has experienced growth of more than 20%. One pastor who had 50 members when he began his weekly trips to the Here's Life Center has seen 200% increase in 12 months' time.

The pastor of Davao's Toril Evangelical Church of the Christian and Missionary Alliance received Campus Crusade's training two years ago during a pastor's management training conference. The year following this training, he personally shared Christ with more than 200 people. He then trained key laymen in his 150-member church. The first two months afterwards, his church members shared the gospel with 400 individuals. The Toril Evangelical Church membership has not increased – for a good reason. Four months after they underwent this training, their first daughter church of 85 members was established! In the next six months they started two additional daughter churches.

Convinced that training does make a difference, this pastor again underwent Campus Crusade's training during the first session at the Davao Here's Life Center. Through the example of his church and his personal encouragement, five other pastors from his denomination attended with him. Now, two of these pastors, at the request of their leadership, have become instructors of the evangelism classes in two of their denomination's Bible Schools.

The curriculum for the classes are the three levels of Campus Crusade for Christ training in evangelism and discipleship. First the pastors train the students in how to share Christ with others and how to conduct follow up sessions. Then, at their request the local Campus Crusade staff teach several sessions on how to teach others to share Christ and follow up the new believers. As a result, when these students graduate from the Bible schools, they are fully equipped to train the people in evangelism in the churches where they are assigned.

To help further meet the need for more advanced training, our movement is operating Great Commission Training Centers in the Philippines, Korea, Taiwan (ROC), Singapore, Malaysia, Indonesia and India.

Also, in September, 1981, the first Asian extension of the International Christian Graduate University School of Theology will open in Baguio City, Philippines. The School of Theology will serve our staff across Asia and the Pacific, and other extensions will be added in the years to come.

The Lord Jesus commanded those who love Him to go into all the world and make disciples. As we obey His command to be His witnesses and to make disciples in the power of the Holy Spirit, we can be assured of a great spiritual awakening and of growth in the organized church.

But how is an ordinary Christian like our Nepal director able to lead a charge through the Himalayan Mountains and successfully reach his goal of taking the gospel message across his country? How is a Bishop in India, who has dreamed for years of evangelizing his diocese, suddenly able to do it? Training makes the difference.

When ordinary Christians as well as strategic church leaders personally learn how to walk by faith in the power of the Holy Spirit and how to share their faith effectively with others, and are then presented with a workable strategy to reach their neighborhood, city, nation or world with the powerful message of Jesus Christ, things happen! Lives are transformed, geographic awakenings occur and the church grows. And it is training that makes the difference!

CHAPTER ELEVEN

An Awakening Is Only The Beginning

God has done incredible things across Asia and the Pacific in the last few years. Fireseeds have burst into flame as thousands of Christians have become involved in sharing God's love with everyone in their spheres of influence, and have then enlarged their borders to distant and difficult areas. As they have been faithful to do this, God has been able to use their lives in mighty and supernatural ways.

Many who read this book will have an increased desire to become a part of what my associates and I believe to be a worldwide awakening to the gospel. If through what you have read, you have been motivated to begin, or to expand, your own personal ministry, take action now.

As you consider your personal involvement in helping to reach the world for Christ, I'm sure you will benefit from a challenge Dr. Kim frequently gives in Korea. He asks five questions.

(1) *Is it God's will?*
Is it God's will for you to be involved in helping to fulfill the Great Commission? We know that the Great Commission was God's idea. He commanded it, so naturally He wants our involvement.

(2) *Since He is willing, is He able?*
Yes, God is able to do what He has commanded. Jesus asked a blind man, "Do you believe I am able to do this?" The blind man

answered, "Yes." Because of his faith, Jesus gave him sight. Jesus has promised to honor your faith in the same way. God is not only willing – He is also able to use you.

(3) *Where shall I start?*

Here and now! Right where you are, begin to expect Him to use you. Begin today. God may desire you to serve Him in another place or another country, but He first wants you to be effective where you are. Do you have a plan for your involvement? Are you trained for your involvement?

(4) *How can I do it?*

Through the power of the Holy Spirit. The Bible is full of beautiful promises concerning what God can do through you. A favorite promise is, "'Not by might nor by power, but by My Spirit,' says the Lord of hosts" (Zechariah 4:6). You can do anything that is in accordance with God's will, through the indwelling power of the Holy Spirit.

(5) *Whom shall He send?*

Isaiah said, "Here am I, Lord, send me." Simply say, "Lord, here I am. Send me... to my neighbor or around the world."

Many statistics have been presented in this book and I would like to try to bring them all together in this chapter, so that you can rejoice with us for the great things God has done, giving Him all praise and glory. As you view these statistics, please keep in mind that each figure represents a human soul.

HERE'S LIFE CAMPAIGNS

Conducted in Hong Kong, India, Indonesia, Japan, Macau, Malaysia, Papua New Guinea, Philippines, Singapore, South Korea, Sri Lanka, Taiwan (ROC) and Thailand, since 1976:

Total made aware that new life can be found in Jesus Christ	176,000,000
Estimated decisions for Christ	3,770,673

"JESUS" FILM SHOWINGS IN 1980

Shown in Burma, Fiji, India, Indonesia, Macau, Malaysia, Micronesia, Nepal, Papua New Guinea, Philippines, South Korea, Solomon Islands, Sri Lanka, Tonga, Thailand, Vanuatu (New Hebrides):

Total attendance	10,396,310
Estimated decisions for Christ	4,691,436
Number of showings	5,775

Average attendance per showing	1,800
(Does not include television showings)	

LITERATURE DISTRIBUTION STRATEGIES IN 1980

Number of pieces distributed	14,257,581

OTHER STRATEGIES IN 1980

Total number exposed	4,922,264
Estimated decisions for Christ	509,173

RADIO MINISTRY IN 1980

Population area broadcasting into	1,628,000,000
Number of letters received	10,246
Indicated decisions for Christ	3,426

HERE'S LIFE, KOREA-'80 WORLD EVANGELIZATION CRUSADE

Estimated decisions for Christ during Here's Life campaign	1,000,000
Estimated decisions for Christ during '80 World Evangelization Crusade	1,500,000
Estimated number who prayed to be filled with the Holy Spirit by faith during '80 World Evangelization Crusade	1,800,000
Estimated number who pledged themselves for foreign missionary service	300,000
Total cumulative attendance, all meetings	16,350,000

CAMPUS CRUSADE FOR CHRIST STAFF GIVING LEADERSHIP TO THESE STRATEGIES IN 44 COUNTRIES OF ASIA AND THE PACIFIC

National staff	898
International staff	172
Associate staff	833
Employees	122
Paid film team members	683
TOTAL	2,708

(This total does not include the hundreds of volunteers who worked for many weeks in the villages showing the film, "Jesus.")

The estimated number of those indicating decisions for Christ through these various strategies totals more than 11 million people. And this is just the beginning. As the film teams gain momentum, it is estimated that nearly 100 million people in Asia and the Pacific region will see the film, "Jesus," in 1981.

Add to this the many other strategies which will be continued, and it becomes evident that the unbelievable acts of the Holy Spirit accomplished during 1980 are only the dawning of what He plans to do during the exciting years ahead.

Christians possess the message of truth – the only truth which sets man free from the bondage of sin and death, and promises abundant life on earth and eternal life with God. God is willing and able to use your time, talent and treasure in such a way that the maximum number of people will receive Christ through your life.

Are you willing to begin here and now to become a "fireseed" in your sphere of influence? Are you willing to say, "Lord, here am I. Send me!" and trust Him to use you to help create a spiritual awakening? An awakening is only the beginning of what He wants to do through your life, and through the lives of others around the world.